Outside the Hospital

The Delivery of Health Care in Non-Hospital Settings

**Don Griffin,
MBA, MS, JD, FACHE**

Polly Griffin

JONES AND BARTLETT PUBLISHERS
Sudbury, Massachusetts
BOSTON   TORONTO   LONDON   SINGAPORE

World Headquarters

Jones and Bartlett
Publishers
40 Tall Pine Drive
Sudbury, MA 01776
978-443-5000
info@jbpub.com
www.jbpub.com

Jones and Bartlett
Publishers Canada
6339 Ormindale Way
Mississauga, Ontario
L5V 1J2
Canada

Jones and Bartlett
Publishers International
Barb House,
Barb Mews
London W6 7PA
United Kingdom

Jones and Bartlett's books and products are available through most bookstores and online book-sellers. To contact Jones and Bartlett Publishers directly, call 800-832-0034, fax 978-443-8000, or visit our website www.jbpub.com.

Substantial discounts on bulk quantities of Jones and Bartlett's publications are available to cor-porations, professional associations, and other qualified organizations. For details and specific discount information, contact the special sales department at Jones and Bartlett via the above contact information or send an email to specialsales@jbpub.com.

This publication is designed to provide accurate and authoritative information in regard to the Subject Matter covered. It is sold with the understanding that the publisher is not engaged in render-ing legal, accounting, or other professional service. If legal advice or other expert assistance is required, the service of a competent professional person should be sought.

Production Credits
Publisher: Michael Brown
Production Director: Amy Rose
Associate Editor: Katey Birtcher
Production Editor: Tracey Chapman
Production Assistant: Roya Millard
Marketing Manager: Sophie Fleck
Manufacturing and Inventory Control Supervisor: Amy Bacus
Composition: Auburn Associates, Inc.
Cover Design: Kate Ternullo
Cover Image: Top photo: © Photos.com; Middle photo: courtesy of Tom Watanabe/U.S. Navy;
    Bottom photo: © Photodisc; Background photo © Lynn Watson/ShutterStock, Inc.
Printing and Binding: Malloy, Inc.
Cover Printing: Malloy, Inc.

Library of Congress Cataloging-in-Publication Data
Griffin, Don, 1949-
    Outside the hospital : the delivery of health care in non-hospital settings / Don Griffin, Polly Griffin.
        p. ; cm.
    Includes bibliographical references and index.
    ISBN-13: 978-0-7637-4504-2 (pbk. : alk. paper)
    ISBN-10: 0-7637-4504-9 (pbk. : alk. paper) 1. Ambulatory medical care. I. Griffin, Polly. II. Title.
    [DNLM: 1. Delivery of Health Care—methods. 2. Ambulatory Care—methods. W 84 G851o 2009]
    RA974.G76 2009
    362.12—dc22

                                                                          2008011538

6048
Printed in the United States of America
12 11 10 09 08   10 9 8 7 6 5 4 3 2 1

Table of Contents

Acknowledgments

Once again, to my dad, Richard Griffin, from whom all knowledge and wisdom springs.

To the faculty at Trinity, especially to Dr. Mary Stefyl, who continues to inspire students and others with her work, leadership, and teaching.

Many thanks to Mike Brown and the staff at Jones and Bartlett for again having faith in me and allowing this continued undertaking.

And finally, to my wife and coauthor, Polly: It is through your research and writing that so much of this is possible.

About the Authors

DON GRIFFIN, MBA, MS, JD, FACHE

After receiving (in the words of his father) "more degrees than a thermometer," Don spent 20 years managing healthcare organizations, including being the CEO of a regional medical center in Texas. He also practiced law in Texas and Oklahoma, generally as counsel to healthcare professionals, and was a professor at two major universities, teaching graduate courses in healthcare economics, health law, bioethics, and strategic planning.

Don and his wife and co-author Polly have lived abroad for several years. Don has been the CEO of hospitals in the United States, China, the United Arab Emirates, and was advisor for 3 years to the Saudi Arabian government on healthcare planning and improving the quality of their healthcare services.

POLLY GRIFFIN

Polly is a gifted and dedicated researcher to whom much of this work should be credited.

Introduction

Health care in America is at a crossroads. As I write in early 2008, Democrats are leaning toward a universal healthcare system, Republicans toward individual assistance through tax credits or health savings accounts. Both parties agree that health spending is out of hand, care is not delivered to everyone, and something must be done. (They agree on little else.)

Health care has recently evolved from the traditional and complex, inpatient hospital setting to a point where most care is diagnosed and delivered outside the walls of hospitals. For example, consumers today are better educated and routinely use the Internet to research their malady and then explore a plethora of treatments. These can range from primary care providers who might be allopathic (MD) or osteopathic (DO) physicians to chiropractors, podiatrists, optometrists, or dentists. The consumer can choose from a variety of home test kits that may be purchased in a neighborhood pharmacy or they may again go online and order a self-test kit by next-day delivery. Consumers may query and seek services from a "virtual" primary care healthcare provider found at the end of their keyboard. They may periodically experience the convenience of a visiting home healthcare provider. Further, services sought outside the hospital might be outpatient imaging, outpatient laboratory testing, or even outpatient surgery. Other services might be to facilitate their pregnancy, to perform dialysis at home or in a center, or to simply find relief from a common allergy or their chronic pain. In any event, most care and healthcare services today are provided in non-traditional settings, *outside* of the hospital.

This text has as its central goal to familiarize all healthcare students and general readers with the numerous options and forms of non-hospital healthcare delivery. Part I of the text presents the traditional form that health care has taken and then moves to newer methods in the delivery of care. In Part II, the reader is guided through current methods of diagnosing health problems such as outpatient imaging centers, outpatient laboratories, and home diagnostic kits available from the Internet or over-the-counter in many retail pharmacies. Part III hosts a wide array of treatment options for acute care problems, ranging from hearing, speaking, seeing, and physical rehabilitation to problems of the mind, sleep-related illnesses (or rather the inability to sleep), and issues with weight loss and preventing exotic travel-related illnesses. Part IV concludes the work by illustrating the outpatient treatment of chronic illnesses, from HIV, dialysis, and oncology to long-term, palliative, and hospice care.

Part I

Traditional Care: Hospitals and Health Care in the United States

Chapter 1

Hospitals and Spiraling Healthcare Costs

Key Terms

Acute care   Non-proprietary

Average length of stay (ALOS)   Outpatient

Hospitals   Proprietary

INTRODUCTION

Once upon a time, hospitals provided care almost exclusively; if people were sick, they either stayed home or were "hospitalized." Today, the rate of hospitalization and the actual number of hospitals is decreasing as more and more services are being provided in **outpatient** care settings. Before the reader is introduced to numerous forms of outpatient care, to form a comparison between traditional inpatient care and the prevalent outpatient trends, we provide a quick overview of American hospitals.

TYPES OF HOSPITALS AND COMMUNITY HOSPITAL STATISTICS

Hospitals take numerous forms, such as federal (military hospitals, the Veterans Administration, or the Indian Health Service), state and municipal hospitals (hospital districts, county hospitals, or city hospitals), religious based (Catholic, Jewish, Methodist, etc.), or even specialty hospitals (women's, children's, or psychiatric). Hospitals usually provide short term (less than 25 days) or acute care. They can be small, serving rural areas, sometimes with 25 beds or less, or large, such as 800-bed centers delivering sophisticated and advanced levels of trauma care. Hospitals may also be physician-owned or a combination with a religious group; also, they may be **proprietary** (for-profit) or **non-proprietary** (non-profit), which is usually determined by the Internal Revenue Service.

Though it would appear from Table 1-1 that hospital admissions grew from 29,252,000 in 1970 to 35,239,000 in 2005, this is misleading. After adjusting for population increase, we see that admissions per population actually declined from approximately 160 per thousand to approximately 112 per thousand, and this is in spite of an aging U.S. population.

The number of hospitals also decreased during this time period, the number of beds per thousand decreased, and the **average length of stay (ALOS)** decreased. The alarming factor is the cost per day and the cost per stay for hospitalization. For the same time period it has literally skyrocketed.

In sharp contrast, the number of outpatient visits has increased, as has the number of outpatient visits per member of the population (Table 1-2).

Table 1-1 Selected Characteristics of All Hospitals With 100+ Beds

Characteristics	1980	1990	2000	2005
No. of hospitals	6,965	6,649	5,810	5,756
Beds (000)	992.0	929.4	823.6	802.3
Admissions (000)	36,143	31,181	33,089	35,239
Admits/thousand	159.6	125.4	117.6	112.0
Average length of stay (days)	7.6	7.2	5.8	5.6
Cost per day ($)	245	687	1,149	1,522
Cost per stay ($)	1,851	4,927	6,649	8,793

Source: Data from Statistical Abstracts of the United States, various years; National Center for Health Statistics and Health, United States, 2003: With Chartbook on Trends in the Health of Americans, 2003, Tables 95, 106, and 122.

Table 1-2 Growth in Outpatient Visits

	1970	2000	2005
Outpatient visits	133,545,000	592,700,000	673,700,000
Visits/person/year	0.66	1.89	2.1

Source: Data from AHA Hospital Statistics, 2007 edition and prior years.

Table 1-3 Number of Ambulatory Surgery Centers, 1997–2003

1997	1998	1999	2000	2001	2002	2003
2,462	2,644	2,786	3,028	3,371	3,597	3,735

Source: Data from MedPAC, Report to Congress, July 2004.

WHY OUTPATIENT PROCEDURES ARE GROWING

To further demonstrate this trend away from hospitals and toward outpatient care, one clear example is the growth of ambulatory surgery centers. In a recent short period (6 years) the number of centers increased by 50% (Table 1-3).

CHAPTER SUMMARY

The number of hospitals in the United States has been declining during the last 30 years, as has the number of admissions per person. The average length of stay has also declined. Costs, however, continue to spiral upward. Because of advances in technology that have led to quicker and less invasive procedures, coupled with increased pressure from third-party payers (Medicare, Medicaid, insurance companies), health trends have seen outpatient procedures trump that of hospitalization.

CHAPTER REVIEW

1. Why have inpatient hospitalizations decreased during the last 30 years?
2. Why have outpatient procedures increased dramatically?
3. What impact do physician-owned services have on the hospitals within their community? To protect themselves financially, should these hospitals form partnership relationships with these physicians?
4. What are several ways to classify hospitals?
5. What is the trend regarding the average length of stay in **acute care** hospitals? Why?
   (One interesting trend is that hospitals are removing physicians from their hospital's staff if they are found to be in economic competition with the hospital. This could be in the form of starting, sharing in, or referring to outpatient imaging centers or surgery centers.)

Discussion: As the baby boomer demographic bubble ages, how long might the trend toward outpatient care continue?

Chapter 2

The Physician's Office: Both a Primary Care Provider and the Gatekeeper for Other Types of Health Care

Key Terms	
Allopathic doctors	Medical Group
American College of	Management Association
Healthcare Executives (ACHE)	(MGMA)
Back office	Medicaid
Certified nurse practitioner	Medicare
Front office	Osteopathic doctors
Health Insurance Portability and	Physician assistant
Accountability Act (HIPAA)	Primary care provider

INTRODUCTION

The general practitioner or **primary care provider** is many times referred to as the "gatekeeper of the medical system." The general physician, practitioner, doctor, or primary care provider may simply answer questions or address concerns the patient may have or may refer the patient to a specialist, order a battery of tests or images, or prescribe medications. In any event, the primary care physician is usually the central point of entry into the healthcare system for all phases of health.

WHAT IS A PRIMARY CARE PROVIDER AND ARE THERE DIFFERENT TYPES?

Primary care physicians are those trained in general practice, family practice, internal medicine, obstetrics and gynecology, and pediatrics. To be referred to as

7

a specialist in any of the foregoing fields, the doctor had to do a residency and then sit for a special examination; upon passing the physician is referred to as "board certified."

More minor "general care" may be delivered by other allied health professionals. These professionals can be a **certified nurse practitioner,** a registered nurse with a master's degree and additional training in the diagnosis and treatment of common problems, or a **physician assistant,** formally trained to assist a physician in the practice of medicine and working under the supervision of a physician or surgeon.

MDs and DOs

To this point, only general practitioners have been mentioned. However, they are different types of general practitioners: medical doctors (MDs) or, even more properly, **allopathic doctors** and **osteopathic doctors** (DOs). Both are physicians, but they have similarities and differences:

- Similarities
  - Both MD and DO applicants have 4 years of undergraduate education, usually with a heavy emphasis in science, usually biology and chemistry.
  - Both MDs and DOs complete 4 years of medical school.
  - After medical school, both DOs and MDs may specialize in areas such as surgery, obstetrics, and radiology.
  - Both DOs and MDs must pass a state licensing examination, very often finding themselves sitting next to each other and taking the same examination.
  - Both usually practice in the same licensed and accredited hospitals.
- Differences
  - DOs usually take a more general or holistic approach, whereas MDs more often become specialists.
  - DOs receive extra training in the musculoskeletal system and are more likely to manipulate the patient in a therapeutic manner.

THE PHYSICIAN'S OFFICE

The medical practitioner's office is usually organized into the **front office** (waiting and reception, intake coordinator, appointments, billing, insurance verification, and sometimes a practice manager) and the **back office** (measurements area, laboratory, imaging, examination rooms, and consultation with the physician). Each function is discussed below.

Before the Appointment

Choosing the Physician

Many researchers marvel at how little thought and time goes into such an important and critical decision as choosing one's doctor. The physician, who can sometimes determine the health or even save the very life of the patient, is many times chosen because a friend of the patient referred the patient to the doctor with statements such as, "You will love this guy, his kids go to school with our kids, and all the magazines in the waiting room are usually current." More research and care might be taken to choose carpet color. At other times the prospective patient moves to a new town and simply searches the yellow pages to find a nearby doctor, relying on who happened to construct the telephone book marketing layout ad. In yet other cases, the patient has limited choices, constricted by which physicians may be in his or her insurance network of providers. At other times, prospective patients may choose to call the local medical society for a referral to a particular type of specialist.

Making the Appointment

After choosing the physician, the patient usually phones for an appointment. He or she inquires if the physician is accepting new patients and if the physician takes a particular brand of insurance. The intake coordinator inquires as to why the patient wishes to see the physician and how soon the appointment is desired. After checking the physician's schedule, a suitable appointment is arranged.

During the Appointment

The Front Office

After the appointment is secured, the patient travels to the physician's office and then enters the waiting area. This may be pleasant with a flowered walkway, current periodicals, and smiling staff; or it may be on the umpteenth floor of an office building, with a sickly crowded waiting room and harried staff members. It is surprising to many patients that physicians give so little thought to the hospitality aspect of their office.

The patient is usually asked to register, to relate a lengthy family and medical history, and to complete insurance forms. He or she will sign a **Health Insurance Portability and Accountability Act (HIPAA)** form and also a consent form for treatment. The intake coordinator will want to know the form of payment the patient plans to use (**Medicare, Medicaid,** third-party insurance, self-payment), and a paragraph on the form will state that in the event of rejection by the third-party insurance company, the patient is still responsible for the bill. In most instances, the patient will pay an insurance copayment or must meet his or her insurance deductible for the office visit.

In the waiting area there may be a television, coffee or chilled beverages, games for kids to play, overhead music, and magazines to read. Also the patient will probably wait beyond the time of the appointment.

The Back Office

When the patient is finally called (and names should not be used due to HIPAA confidentiality requirements), they are taken to a measurements room to have his or her height and weight measured, blood pressure taken, and, if diabetic, his or her finger stuck to measure the current blood sugar level. The patient will then be quizzed by the nurse aid, physician's assistant, or certified nurse practitioner to record the reasons the patient is visiting the physician.

After the interview, notes are placed in the patient's medical record, and the patient is taken to one of several exam rooms to await the physician. This is actually an efficient way to see patients; each patient is prepped, interviewed, and placed in waiting rooms and the doctor merely moves from room to room, wasting little time and maximizing the number of people she or he treats each hour. (This is especially true when one considers how medicine was practiced just 4 decades ago with house calls. Gone are those days when one could simply phone the doctor and request a house call because the patient was too ill to go to the doctor's office.) In today's busy world, the impracticality of that type of doctor–patient relationship does not exist; most doctors will never spend "windshield time" driving from patient house to patient house.

The Physician

After yet another wait, the physician will enter the examination room, always accompanied by a nurse to make notes, hand supplies, or take additional measurements (and to protect the physician from later acquisitions of impropriety). During the discussion with the patient and the diagnosis, the physician will carefully tap, prod, push, peer, cajole, or otherwise investigate the patient's complaint, trying to rule out maladies and then determine what is causing the discomfort, sickness, or complaint.

More tests may be ordered. An image (x-ray, computed tomography, ultrasound, or magnetic resonance image) may be needed to assist in the diagnosis, or additional laboratory tests may be needed. Medications may be ordered, usually for an allergy or to relieve pain. The illness or pain may be beyond the scope of the physician and a specialist is needed; therefore, a referral is generated and a call is made to schedule the patient to see a more specialized provider.

After the Appointment

When the patient exits the office, a billing clerk, receptionist, or even the original intake coordinator will review the physician's report and, if necessary, make an appointment for a follow-up visit. If the physician is astute, a call will be made to the patient in a few days to elicit patient satisfaction information.

PROFESSIONAL PRACTICE ADMINISTRATORS

In the old days, a physician was boss of the practice; after all, he or she owned it. Physicians would hire and fire, buy supplies, take money to the bank and make the deposit, or one of their relatives would assist, such as their wife, son, or daughter.

Often, the practice would grow managers internally. For example, a person is hired to answer the telephones, but as a few years pass he or she becomes the insurance verification person or the billing person. A few more years pass and the person grows in trust and assumes more and more duties and evolves into the medical practice administrator, handling all business affairs for the physician. Although having many years of on-the-job training, the weakness of this model may be that the person who grew into the job may lack formal education in areas such as marketing, accounting, or management.

Therefore a new opportunity has risen for those interested in a career in healthcare administration. Instead of setting a goal to become the administrator of a hospital, many graduate students are finding quicker satisfaction, less competition, and nearly equal salary in the field of medical practice administration. These people finish graduate school in healthcare administration and sometimes walk into a position managing a physician's practice. They may have MBA skills, understand marketing and accounting, and, though not experienced in the front and back offices, lend their business skills to successfully managing the practice.

Often, physicians practice together, share facilities and employees, and divide overhead, linked together into an independent practice association, a partnership, or some other form of group practice. Members of these non-solo practices want to arrive at work, see patients, and then go home. They became doctors to treat patients, not to interview billing clerks, buy new office equipment, or attend advertising workshops. In contrast, the medical practice administrator is hired to manage the business side of the practice and is paid well to do so.

This career model is recommended for those students who are interested in quicker advancement as an alternative to hospital administration. The professional group for hospital administrators is the **American College of Healthcare Executives (ACHE);** an equally prestigious professional group that is more focused on medical practices is the **Medical Group Management Association (MGMA)** and its educational wing, the American College of Medical Practice Executives. Jobs are more plentiful, students from graduate programs are more competitive in the workplace than those individuals who have worked in practices but are not formally educated, and salaries are higher earlier in the individual's career (though the salary of a hospital administrator may outpace the medical group administrator in the long run).

Both the ACHE and the MGMA organizations have professional advancement criteria; demand attendance in workshops to gain credits to advance; have written examinations covering topics such as accounting, law, management of information systems, and human resources; and have many thousands of members. Perhaps the biggest advantage of membership in either organization is the list of hundreds of jobs that each organization displays. The author recommends membership in either or both as a way to professionally advance in either respective field.

CHAPTER SUMMARY

Primary care physicians are the gatekeepers of health care. These physicians, either MDs or DOs, are usually the first person to examine, diagnose, and offer treatment to the patient. From here the patient may receive further testing, imaging, or see a specialist for a more in-depth examination and care. Healthcare administration students may choose to pursue a career in assisting physicians in the efficient management of their practice.

CHAPTER REVIEW

1. How does a physician become "board certified"?
2. What is the difference between a DO and an MD? Are they both physicians? What is the difference in the state medical examination that each takes?
3. What is HIPAA, and what is its impact on the patient and the physician's office?
4. Why is consent for treatment absolutely necessary for each patient and each visit?
5. Why is follow-up after the office visit important to the physician's practice?

Discussion: A friend of yours has just moved into the area and asks you to recommend a physician. You haven't been there long enough to see a physician yourself. What do you say, and how would you advise your friend to find an appropriate doctor?

Chapter 3

Urgent Care Centers: "The Doc in the Box"

Key Terms	
Ancillary services	Urgent care centers
Convenience clinics	

INTRODUCTION

Urgent care centers are one of the most rapidly expanding sectors of the American healthcare industry. These are designed to be rapid access outlets for walk-in patients who require timely treatment of injuries or illnesses that are not severe enough to necessitate a trip to a hospital emergency department. These consumers do not want to wait for a scheduled appointment with their primary care physician and most often find the urgent care center quick, convenient, and affordable.

HISTORY

Urgent care centers first began operation about 30 years ago but did not see a rapid expansion until the mid-1990s. It is thought within the healthcare industry that urgent care centers were not accepted by consumers initially because there was no marketing for the centers; consumers simply did not know what services were available, what could be expected, or how much they cost. They simply put their trust in the local hospital's emergency department. An additional reason for the failed expansion is that hospitals were buying the centers as potentially profitable **ancillary services** while counting on patients to use the urgent care centers as an entry point into the hospital. Hospitals viewed their centers as a downstream part of the marketing chain, the hospital believing that for every group of patients,

13

a few would need hospitalization. Because of high overhead (the centers were managed in the same manner as hospitals), the profitability of these centers did not evolve and in many cases they were closed.

"BUILD THEM AND THEY WILL COME"

With an understanding of public demand and an entrepreneurial spirit, many primary care and emergency physicians who are weary of "24/7" health care move into urgent care center practices. Burned out by the burden of traditional medical practices and looking for a change from the demanding schedules of office/hospital practice, some doctors, independently or collaboratively with hospitals, are opening new centers and fueling the growth of urgent care centers. These doctors are finding a new role in medicine by emphasizing high-quality care that is convenient. Marketing the urgent care center is similar to that of a 20-minute oil change center—"convenience, convenience, convenience" at a reasonable price.

In addition, many hospital emergency departments now operate urgent care centers that are often adjacent to or within the hospital facility. Patients can go directly to the center or may be assessed in the emergency department through a triage system; if determined to be a low acuity patient (lower than requiring care in a hospital emergency department), they can be sent to the urgent care center for treatment. This then frees the emergency department doctor for "true" emergencies. The new patient would most likely remain in the hospital's treatment system and, if needed, would be provided continuing care of a more comprehensive nature, resulting in a healthier patient.

In a new trend, more and more urgent care centers are specializing in pediatric care. Instead of being in direct competition, they are working in concert with primary care pediatric practices. In many instances, these pediatric urgent care centers are open only during hours that pediatric physician's offices are closed, such as evenings, weekends, and on holidays.

SCOPE OF URGENT CARE

Although all urgent care centers can treat many problems seen in the primary care physician's office, they can also offer services not normally available in those offices. Examples include:

- X-ray facilities for basic radiology imaging in the treatment of minor fractures or for chest x-rays
- In-house laboratory departments for routine blood tests and other diagnostic procedures to prevent the inconvenience of sending to off-site laboratories

- Procedure rooms to set minor fractures and suture average lacerations
- Prepackaged prescription services (medicines can arrive in prefilled packages, eliminating a trip to the pharmacy to fill a prescription [this is dependent on state law])
- On-site physical therapy

No continuing supervision is given for chronic conditions.

Minor Injuries, Illnesses, Routine Care, and Diagnostics

A visit to an urgent care center would be appropriate for any of the following:

- Minor injuries
  - Sprains, strains, minor fractures
  - Minor injuries associated with automobile accidents
  - First- or second-degree burns
  - Minor eye injuries
- Minor illnesses
  - Fevers
  - Abdominal pain
  - Sore throat
  - Asthma
  - Ear or eye infections
- Routine care
  - Allergy injections
  - Sports and school physicals
  - Flu vaccines
- Diagnostic testing and imaging
  - Urinalysis
  - X-rays
  - Electrocardiograms
  - Pregnancy tests

Visits would not be appropriate for conditions that are life-threatening such as chest pain, (which could signal a heart attack), stroke, difficulty in breathing, severe bleeding or pain, loss of consciousness, or when there is any doubt about the seriousness of an illness or injury. Patients should then visit the nearest hospital emergency room or call 911 for help.

CONVENIENCE AND LOCATION

Urgent care centers are normally found in urban neighborhoods, in retail shopping centers, or in freestanding clinic buildings. Most are convenient and easy to locate, with urgent care centers located in most American cities and often with multiple locations. Consumers are usually elated that there is little or no waiting period to be treated for a minor injury or illness. They can drop in, be treated, pick up medicines, and go home with a feeling of relief in a short period of time. Gone are the long waits in the primary care physician's office (if one can even secure an appointment) or in a crowded hospital emergency department where a patient may wait for hours to receive the same care that can be provided in an urgent care center in less than an hour and at a very fraction of the price.

WHO PAYS?

Most health insurance plans, including Medicare and Medicaid, cover urgent care, but patients should check their plans to confirm coverage for services and acquire prior authorization when necessary. In most cases, if a patient in a health maintenance organization (HMO) insurance plan contacts his or her primary care physician and is instead told to go to the urgent care center, he or she will pay for the visit directly or will pay a regular office copayment. Some health plans are now charging a higher copay to consumers who use the emergency department for non-emergency care such as bronchitis, ear infection, sinusitis, and strep throat. A call to one's primary care physician or health plan's hotline could help to determine whether to seek care at an urgent care center or in the local hospital emergency department.

It is rare that an urgent care center advertises that it will treat anyone regardless of insurance coverage or ability to pay. Usually urgent care centers are proprietary in nature, though at a fraction of the emergency department cost.

A few urgent care centers offer a discount membership plan to patients and their families who are without medical insurance. Although it is *not* insurance, the plan does offer urgent care at affordable rates with proper identification and a membership card at the time services are provided. A reduced fee may even be offered to clients who have high insurance deductibles or perhaps have had a lapse in their health insurance coverage.

For employees who suffer on-the-job injuries that can be treated as minor, workers' compensation may be filled when the treatment is delivered, and the state usually accepts the treatment within the workers' compensation claim process.

CUSTOMER SERVICE AND SATISFACTION

Extended hours, enhanced customer service, and low cost are positive characteristics of urgent care centers. There is an increased emphasis on customer service with some urgent care centers, allowing patients to register online through providing required information before going to the center. This advanced one-time registration may keep patients and their families coming often by lowering one of the barriers to entering the center's system. Some urgent care centers are offering to send reports to primary care physicians that describe visits patients have made to the center, yet another step in promoting customer service.

Many corporations and city municipalities are utilizing urgent care centers for occupational health. Employer-paid services include workers' compensation cases, employment physical examinations, and drug screening. Not only are the centers more convenient for employees and potential employees, they are more cost effective for employers than would be a primary care physician. Urgent care centers can reduce the time spent away from work for medical appointments thereby saving the employer money.

HOURS OF OPERATION AND STAFFING

As previously stated, most urgent care centers are open for extended hours. Typical hours are 8 a.m. to 8 p.m. Monday through Friday and 11 a.m. to 5 p.m. Saturday and Sunday; other centers provide limited hours on holidays.

Normally, at least one physician is on duty accompanied by a nurse practitioner or physician assistant. Additionally, there are medical assistants, lab technicians, x-ray technicians, and office staff. The number of staff depends on the size of the urgent care center and the patient load. Some smaller rural remote centers may have only a nurse practitioner or physician assistant and staff that perform more than one job, from registering patients to giving injections to completing the billing process. These centers, however, still have a physician available for consultation and to review care.

CONVENIENCE CLINICS

The latest offering in health care for the most basic medical problems at economical prices are **convenience clinics,** which are set up in retail and grocery chain stores. With multiple facilities, the chains have an advantage of consolidating costs to maximize profit, have name recognition through mass marketing, and, with increased visibility, have created a sense of "reliability" to consumers.

Instead of a physician on duty, convenience clinics are most often staffed by registered nurse practitioners (registered nurses with master's degrees who are allowed to prescribe medications) or with physician assistants who are qualified to evaluate, diagnose, and prescribe medications for common illnesses and to provide some vaccinations and screening as listed below:

- Common illnesses: allergies, bronchitis, ear infections, sore throat
- Additional treatment: laryngitis, swimmer's ear
- Skin infections: athlete's foot, cold sores, insect bites, minor burns, rashes
- Screenings: pregnancy, allergy testing (18+)
- Vaccines: flu, hepatitis B (adult or child), measles, mumps, rubella

Convenience clinic hours normally coincide with those of the host retail store. Patients outside the scope of services provided at the convenience clinic are referred to their physician, urgent care center, or emergency room and are usually not billed if they cannot be treated.

The negative side of convenience clinics is that there is not a physician on site, which creates a lower level of care and results in these clinics not being allowed to operate in some states. It remains to be seen if this limited level of health care will be widely accepted by the public.

FUTURE OF URGENT CARE CENTERS

Will the aging population create new demands for urgent care centers? Will the time it takes to secure an appointment with a primary care physician and/or the waiting time spent in overcrowded hospital emergency departments increase the popularity of urgent care centers? Will the millions of people without health-care insurance look to urgent care centers for affordable acute care? Will the competition between urgent care centers, primary care physicians, and hospital emergency departments make consumers the beneficiaries of improved health care through convenient, quick, and affordable services? It is the author's belief that all of these questions will be answered with a resounding 'Yes!'.

CHAPTER SUMMARY

Urgent care centers, a recent trend in the delivery of health care, provide a host of advantages to the consumer over the traditional hospital emergency department, not the least of which are money and time. Convenience clinics are even further on the cutting edge, by providing health care in large retail outlets and at extended hours. These are not a be-all, end-all provision of care, but used appropriately these centers can provide cost savings and the all important time factor.

CHAPTER REVIEW

1. How do urgent care centers differ from hospital emergency departments? List several reasons that are positive and several that are negative.
2. Why are physicians attracted to urgent care practices, as opposed to the traditional family practice model?
3. What factors in society seem to be driving the opening of so many urgent care centers?
4. What care might you seek from an urgent care center? When would you instead choose a hospital emergency department?
5. If a physician assistant or registered nurse practitioner examines and offers treatment to patients, how does the law in your state address the frequency of review by a qualified physician?

Discussion: Should states regulate urgent care centers in a different manner from a physician's office practice or that of a hospital emergency department? Why or why not? Is the delivery of all health care the same, or do some delivery models merit different statutes and regulations?

Chapter 4

The Virtual Doctor's Office

Key Terms

Third-party payers   Virtual office

INTRODUCTION

More and more citizens are seeking medical advice online, weighing options for treatment and researching more in-depth knowledge about their disease. This can be in advance of seeing their physician, whose office visit may take the inconvenient form of the patient (1) booking an appointment, (2) getting dressed up and driving while not feeling well, (3) finding a parking place and even paying to park, and then (4) discovering that the physician encounter itself may be limited to a 10- to 15-minute rushed affair (the limitations most often imposed by financial incentives or the insurance provider). In an alternative form, the patient's Internet research may follow the physician office visit, much in the manner of seeking a second medical opinion. In either event, the Internet is changing the manner in which primary health care is delivered.

In a step beyond the two forms just illustrated (before the physician visit or after the physician visit), many are seeking their physician's knowledge and advice over the Internet in place of *any* office visit. As patients grow confident in their own Internet skills and as an added result of their Internet medical research and evaluation processes, many patients evolve in their thinking and want to avoid sitting in their physician's office at all, where they would be with other sick people and stale magazines and suffer a long wait.

Physicians are very willing to accommodate this new market force and manner of practicing medicine, with many physicians now seizing the opportunity to practice online as both a supplement and complement to their office practice.

ADVANTAGES AND DISADVANTAGES

Offering secure consultations and treatment; charges for simple consultations, diagnosis, and treatment; and sometimes provision of prescriptions for noncomplicated conditions can range from $25 to $50. This may be a real bargain for both parties.

The physician usually creates a website, letting patients and others know of the new offering of more convenient medical services. When logging onto the physician's site, the patient most often finds that the **virtual office** fee can be paid by a debit or a credit card. The patient then completes a thorough and systematic history for any of a long host of complaints. The physician, logging on at a convenient time, scans the list of virtual patients, completing a review of their provided information and deciding which patients may be treated in this manner and which patients need to be contacted for an in-person visit.

If the patient is not treatable online and must visit the physician, a big advantage is that the information is already in the patient's medical record, saving the receptionist, nurse, and doctor valuable time. This preregistration, insurance update, secure bill payment, prescription refills, lab results, and placement directly in the medical record are also, without a doubt, very convenient for the patient.

The physician benefits further because by the patients completing the form by keyboard, their answers are often more comprehensive, accurate, and in better chronological order than a verbal office interview with the patients sitting in their underwear in an exam room, with limited time, with the doctor distracted by other patients and their problems.

Another advantage of virtual medicine is that for many patients, discussion of flatulence, incontinence, or erectile dysfunction is easier when addressing their keyboard and computer than in person with the doctor. This virtual interaction may lead to more honest and comprehensive answers. Also, software questions tend to be non-judgmental, and as the software adjusts itself to the preceding answers, better questions and thus more information may be coaxed from the patient and a better diagnosis delivered.

Most patients using services of this kind already know their physician. Treatment of this nature can be less expensive for the physician because there is reduced office overhead. Treatment for the patient is also less expensive, and parking problems, inclement weather, and scheduling issues are avoided.

Treating patients online may also assist the physician in staying competitive with the increasingly popular simple retail health clinics that treat minor problems. Patients can be treated in the same manner, without leaving their home, and with help from their own physician.

A disadvantage of the virtual office, however, is that **third-party payers** (insurance companies, Medicare, and Medicaid) do not cover these online visits.

CHAPTER SUMMARY

Consumers of health care have grown accustomed to searching the Internet for answers to their maladies, aches, pains, and illnesses, perceived or otherwise. A step beyond this is a visit to their provider, over the Internet, without leaving their homes. The primary care physician can size up the problem, make recommendations, and even have a prescription delivered by only seeing the patient that is at the end of their keyboard, saving time and money for both parties.

CHAPTER REVIEW

1. What forms of healthcare delivery can the Internet provide?
2. What are the advantages and disadvantages of online physician visits?
3. How could third-party payers be persuaded to pay for virtual office visits?

Discussion: Should a physician always be familiar with or know his or her patient before offering medical advice online? What about problems with high blood pressure, chest pain, or skin allergies? Can these be treated without visually encountering the patient? Could home testing equipment, such as blood pressure cuff or a diabetic home testing system, or could even a web-cam, provide necessary information?

Part II

Diagnosing: New Methods and Facilities

Chapter 5

Pharmacies and Home Testing Devices

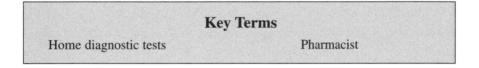

Key Terms	
Home diagnostic tests	Pharmacist

INTRODUCTION

A **pharmacist** is one who dispenses or, more infrequently, compounds and dispenses medications to patients. He or she also provides counseling and drug information such as side effects, interactions, and the correct dosage amounts. In retail operations, the pharmacist may provide assistance to customers in choosing over-the-counter medications and other healthcare supplies. The pharmacist may also give advice about diet, exercise, or stress management. He or she may assist in choosing durable medical equipment and other home care health equipment.

Many pharmacists may own their own retail operations, whereas other pharmacists choose to avoid what they perceive as the headaches of retail work, instead opting for a more professional healthcare setting, choosing to be a hospital employee and advising physicians regarding prescription medications, their contraindications, interactions, and generic substitutes. Other pharmacists may choose to specialize in a medical subset such as oncology, mixing chemotherapy for cancer centers. And still others may own or practice in a geriatric pharmacy setting, focusing on the elderly and other types of long-term care patients. Some pharmacists may work in a drug therapy center, specializing in the rehabilitation of patients with addiction illnesses. Other pharmacists might choose psychopharmacotherapy and spend their time mixing and dispensing drugs to assist and treat patients that are mentally challenged.

In any event, the local pharmacy or retail drug store is our focus; for the consumer it is an important source of medications and information, probably second only to the general practitioner in importance. It is also an important source for the increasingly sophisticated consumer to purchase new and evolving methods of self-diagnosis.

HOME DIAGNOSTIC TESTS

It is interesting that the pharmacy and also the Internet are now becoming a source for an expanded healthcare product, **home diagnostic tests**, including self-testing diagnostic and monitoring devices. These products probably first arose in the form of home pregnancy tests. Because of their popularity, the market looked for new areas for expansion, next moving into diabetes and then cholesterol testing. Recent novel innovations include testing for alcohol use, tobacco use, and recently home hair tests to monitor for illegal drug use. These home test kits, available over the counter at many pharmacies (dependent on state law), are proving less expensive and much more convenient than the alternative trip to a physician's office. Home test kits are often as cheap as the physician office copay or deductible and, of course, are much more convenient than the physician in that no appointment is necessary, home test kits may be purchased at pharmacies usually having 7-day extended hours, and pharmacy locations outnumber the patient's family physician. In addition, spiraling healthcare costs, the recent increased interest in premium health, and a desire for confidentiality and privacy will probably continue to drive the extended use of self-testing kits and self-care.

Advantages and Disadvantages

Healthcare professionals, however, caution about the reliance on these devices. Home test kits do not give treatment advice, only that the person tested is (perhaps) positive or negative for a particular condition. There are no treatment methodologies offered or, worse, no counseling for something of grave importance such as testing positive for HIV. These should be used only as an adjunct to a visit to the doctor, not a replacement for the visit.

Of great importance is the lack of value of the test kit if the person using the kit does not carefully follow the provided instructions. Kits may also prove difficult to use; for example, a kit to predict ovulation by using body temperature may easily be misread, lending uncertainty to the procedure.

Still other kits might be stored incorrectly, either in transit, at the pharmacy, or after purchase. This may cause the kit to deteriorate and become useless. Other kits may lack sensitivity or be prone to false positives (reporting a pregnancy or a disease when it is not a pregnancy or a disease) or, much worse, reporting false negatives (reporting no pregnancy or disease when there is a pregnancy or a disease).

Other problems with home test kits may include food interactions or urine samples collected too early or too late in the day. Besides not correctly following instructions (which could be a function of dexterity), consumers also may not be able to understand the instructions, such as being asked to provide an ml or a dc of a body fluid.

Types of Available Test Kits

Home test kits on the market include testing for the following:

- Alcohol use
- Blood pressure
- Blood type
- Cholesterol
- Diabetes
- Drug use
- Various hazardous chemicals
- Pregnancy
- Infertility
- Tobacco use

Available mail-in laboratory tests include the following:

- Allergies
- DNA
- Drug use from hair samples
- Hepatitis C
- Mold
- Paternity
- Prostate
- Thyroid problems

CHAPTER SUMMARY

Pharmacists can provide a great array of knowledge about health and health care and an irreplaceable expertise in drug use, drug interactions, and contraindications for drug use. Home test kits, if used in the properly prescribed manner, provide a convenient and inexpensive method for consumers to assist themselves in diagnosing illnesses. Used in conjunction with visiting their physician, consumers may find their knowledge and delivery of health care to be better than at any other time in history.

CHAPTER REVIEW

1. Besides retail operations, where else might one find pharmacists working?
2. What are some advantages of home testing kits?
3. What are the limitations of home testing kits?
4. Name two ways to obtain a home testing kit.
5. What are some of the things for which a home testing kit might be used?

Discussion: A friend asks for your advice. It seems your friend, after engaging in unsafe sex, has bought and used an HIV self-testing kit with the results being positive. What advice do you give her about the test, being retested, and possibly seeing her physician?

Chapter 6

Outpatient Laboratories

Key Terms

Direct access testing (DAT)   Outpatient laboratories
Drawing stations

INTRODUCTION

Science and medicine have advanced dramatically in recent years. Thus test samples that were once obtained in physicians' offices are now obtained at more convenient **drawing stations** in medical office buildings or near large physician practices, with transportation couriers picking up specimens at all hours of the day and night and taking them to a central laboratory for processing. Results from the specimen testing are electronically sent to the physician that ordered the test. In summary, the patient is sent by his or her physician to a drawing station and then phones the same physician the next day for the results. The doctor has done nothing except write the order; the laboratory draws, transports, analyzes, and reports the results.

Outpatient laboratories also do a large business with preemployment screenings and on-the-job drug testing. An applicant may be requested to report to a laboratory to produce a specimen as part of the preemployment screening process. Employees who have a major accident or one involving a vehicle may be required to produce a lab specimen for screening of illegal drugs. Many other employees are even selected at random to be screened, with the randomness being a deterrent to stop on- or off-the-job drug use. The federal government also uses such outpatient lab drug testing in many of their departments; an example is air traffic controllers.

DIRECT ACCESS TESTING

Until recently, a healthcare provider was the only one who could order lab work. Now many states are relaxing these standards. Home test kits are available, as seen in Chapter 5, and in several states **direct access testing (DAT)** is allowed. This is a deformalization of health care in the traditional sense, which now allows the patient or consumer to access a laboratory and the results without having to consult or even contact a physician. This will certainly not replace physicians but could propel laboratories to a more prominent place in the healthcare spectrum. Lab personnel do not practice medicine; however, the patient's test results and how they compare to the normal expected range must be at least presented. Patients, consumers, and customers are then on their own to find a healthcare provider to analyze and explain the results and offer, if necessary, a course of treatment.

There are usually four formats of DAT which are:

1. A walk-in laboratory where staff are trained to collect specimens. The patient would then phone the laboratory for the results, using a predetermined patient number to help assist and ensure confidentiality (someone else cannot phone to find out the results).
2. A mail-order test kit where the patient collects his or her own specimen and then sends it in. An example is a cheek swab for HIV, which is mailed to a lab and the results obtained later by mail.
3. Facilities where blood is donated, screened (e.g., for hepatitis or HIV), and then results reported to the person donating.
4. At-home test kits, where the patient produces and then collects the sample, performs the test, interprets the results, and then determines the appropriate response. An example is home pregnancy test kits.

The above developments are most likely driven by cost-reduction measures in health care (removing the physician visit), better informed consumers, convenience (no physician appointment or waiting, no missed time from work, and then no repeating the physician visit process to obtain the results), improved privacy (no stigma when testing for sexually transmitted disease or drug use, and no fear of rejection by an insurance company because of documented results in a medical record), and greater control over one's own health care.

A major disadvantage may be that insurance companies do not always cover the costs of the tests unless the test is ordered by the patient's physician. Another is the potential by the patient of misinterpreting the results. A societal concern may be that contagious and reportable diseases will go unreported, diseases such as HIV. Finally, fraudulent and incompetent laboratory work may take place.

A big feature of DAT is that much of the transaction is done via the Internet (i.e., reading about the test, ordering it, and then seeing the results later online). Important areas of testing are in women's health, diabetes, infectious diseases, and some cardiovascular diseases.

CHAPTER SUMMARY

The trend toward the use of outpatient laboratory testing and services is strong. Patients may be referred by their physician to a host of facilities or may even self-refer, depending on the laws in their state. Patients may provide samples at the laboratory site and then be given results by either their physician or the laboratory itself. Patients may also purchase self-testing kits and return them to the company for testing and results.

Major advantages of outpatient laboratory testing include savings in cost, time, and protected confidentiality. Major disadvantages exist if the patient is not sophisticated in understanding the results or is not counseled as to what next to undertake in treatment.

CHAPTER REVIEW

1. What are some major advantages in outpatient laboratory testing over that of laboratory testing provided by the patient's physician?
2. What are some of the disadvantages in a patient independently being tested at an outpatient laboratory without the assistance of his or her physician?
3. What are the advantages to an employer of retaining the services of an outpatient laboratory?
4. Why do some states not allow self-referral testing by laboratories of patients (i.e., in these select states, a physician must always write an order before the laboratory may perform the test)?
5. What are four forms that direct access testing might take?

Discussion: Should Internet test results be sent directly to a patient or should they be sent only to the patient's physician? Why?

Chapter 7

Outpatient Imaging Centers and Services

Key Terms

Angiography	Mammography
Bone densitometry	Magnetic resonance
Computed tomography (CT)	imaging (MRI)
Electroencephalography (EEG)	Nuclear medicine
Electrocardiography (ECG)	Positron emission
Electromyography (EMG)	tomography (PET)
Fluoroscopy	Ultrasound
Imaging	Virtual colonoscopy

INTRODUCTION

The number of freestanding outpatient **imaging** centers has blossomed and proliferated in the past dozen years. This has largely been driven by better outpatient reimbursement over that of the traditional acute care setting (hospitals), a heightened convenience factor for the patient, physicians who are supportive of the added convenience for their patients, and equipment manufacturers eager to sell more imaging devices.

SERVICES

A plethora of services are available. Depending on the imaging center and what the owners decide to include, there may be many services offered. These services are discussed below to familiarize the reader with the terms, applications of the procedure, and the process.

Mammography

A mammogram is nothing more complicated than an x-ray image taken of the breasts and is used primarily to screen for precancer and cancer. Though breast cancer is the second leading cause of death among women, it can usually be detected in early stages, and thus routine annual imaging is usually recommended for women over 40 years of age. A mammogram is a fast, safe procedure that is normally not painful, although some women may experience discomfort due to the compression of the breasts against the x-ray detector, if that is the method used. (**Magnetic resonance imaging [MRI]** is sometimes used when the patient has silicone breast implants.) The significant benefits of **mammography** in the prevention of cancer far outweigh the discomfort.

The x-ray mammography machine is often used in conjunction with an R2 ImageChecker, which is a computer-aided piece of equipment that spots tiny abnormal changes and calcifications that may have been undetected through self-breast examination or doctor examination. This piece of equipment can result in the detection of about 20% more cancers than the mammogram alone.

Ultrasound

The **ultrasound** machine, sometimes known as a sonogram, uses ultrasonic sound waves to bounce off tissue, producing real-time dimensional images of internal organs, veins and arteries of the legs, or, most commonly, a fetus. This non-invasive imaging device is used by obstetricians, cardiologists, gastroenterologists, neurosurgeons, and a host of physicians in an attempt to detect a range of conditions. Advanced digital ultrasound is totally safe and painless, permitting physicians to view characteristics of anatomy and physiology as they could not before.

Bone Densitometry

Bone densitometry is a relatively safe, noninvasive, radiological test that is used to measure the bone's mineral content and therefore the risk of fracture. Calcium loss (osteoporosis) may accelerate in older adults (women and men) and postmenopausal women who no longer produce estrogen. Bone density involves many factors such as heredity, sex, age, physical activities, and the use of specific medications. Whether one smokes or not is also a factor. This quick, simple procedure, usually performed at the site of the hip, can aid in predicting bone strength. Osteoporosis is a common condition that is the major cause of hip and vertebral fracture in the elderly. Bone densitometry detects early stages of osteoporosis before symptoms are present. The procedure allows for testing the density of bones in the spine, lower arm, thigh, and pelvis and is normally done in a clinic, an imaging diagnostic center, or a hospital. Bone densitometry may also be applied to confirm an existing fracture, calculate chances of future fractures, and establish rate of bone loss.

The primary care physician can explain the procedure to the patient, with no prior preparation being required. The patient is simply placed prone on the density table, and an image is taken of the pelvis at the thickest point. This is compared with what is considered normal or average density to determine if bone loss is occurring in the patient.

Computed Tomography

With **computed tomography (CT),** a beam of ionizing radiation (commonly known as an x-ray) is directed from various angles at the area of the body to be scanned. A high-speed computer programmed with various body tissue absorption capacities then assembles a composite image of a slice of the organ or limb in question. The CT machine can produce images that would be impossible with ordinary x-ray procedures.

The patient lies on a table that is slid into a large device that could be said to resemble a donut hole. When the procedure begins, the patient hears a drumming sound. The technician directs the patient to be very still to produce a clear image. At the conclusion of the procedure, the patient leaves the table and goes home. The staff radiologist examines the image and then dictates a report to be sent to the physician who ordered the study. This physician then speaks to the patient about the image result.

Magnetic Resonance Imaging (MRI)

This device uses no radiation; rather it uses electromagnetic energy to prompt hydrogen atoms to produce signals that are then converted into images of high detail by powerful computers. MRI machines are manufactured in different field strengths such as a 0.5 Tesla, 1.0 Tesla, and 1.5 Tesla. The greater the field strength, the quicker the patient may be imaged, thus shortening the time the patient must lie still.

Because of claustrophobia, about 10% of patients reject the donut-hole device that the MRI resembles; they simply do not feel comfortable in the confined space. For this reason, many patients may be offered a mild sedative or may be given a special pair of prism glasses so that they can view a movie or television program during the procedure. Sometimes, the MRI machine rejects the patient (i.e., the patient is simply too large to fit in the machine). In this case, or in the case of claustrophobia, there are machines that are open; that is, rather than resembling a donut hole, they resemble two horizontal plates held apart by four pillars—the machine is open on all four sides.

Because the MRI machine produces high magnetic fields, patients with ferrous metal within their body may not undertake the procedure. This can include cardiac pacemakers or even tattooed eyeliner. However, because the machine produces no radiation, family members may be in the room during the imaging procedure, provided that they also do not have metal in or on their body.

Fluoroscopy

Basically, **fluoroscopy** is the study of real-time images that are taken with x-rays. The "moving picture" images are sent to a television-type monitor allowing a radiologist/physician to view the body structure in motion. Normally performed on an outpatient basis, a fluoroscopy is used to look at various systems of the body, including respiratory, digestive, and reproductive.

Cardiac catheterization, which is a diagnostic form of fluoroscopy, can be used to determine pressure and blood flow in the heart's chambers, collect blood samples, and examine the arteries for blockage. An evaluation can be done to discover coronary artery disease, valve problems, heart enlargement, or heart abnormalities in newborns.

X-Ray

X-rays are a form of electromagnetic radiation that can pass through the human body as x-ray particles. The x-rays create images that are then recorded onto film or a computer that digitally produces a picture. X-rays are taken by a technician while the patient is prone, standing, or sitting, depending on the type and area of analysis. X-rays are developed or digitally reproduced and then read and evaluated by a radiologist. The use of x-rays poses minimal risk for cancer; risk is offset by the information obtained. If contrast materials are injected or swallowed, allergic reactions may occur in a small percentage of patients. Other contraindications for x-rays are women who are pregnant. The following are useful procedures for x-rays:

- Pelvic x-rays: These x-rays can find problems that result from abdominal pain or perhaps abnormalities in the urinary tract such as kidney stones.
- Gallbladder x-rays: For this procedure a patient is asked to swallow six tablets (one at a time) the night before the procedure. The tablets include a special dye that allows the images to be seen well. Gallbladder x-rays assist in the diagnosing of liver and gallbladder diseases such as gallstones.
- Skull x-rays: These produce images of the bones surrounding the brain, including the facial bones. Whenever there has been head trauma from an accident or any type of injury, an x-ray can be ordered to detect bleeding, increased pressure, or fracture in the skull. It is common to x-ray patients who are suspected to have Alzheimer's disease, seizures, or dementia.

- Joint x-rays: Most often x-rays of the joints include the complete knee, hip, or wrist. These are performed for suspected fractures, arthritis, tumors, or inflammation of the bone due to infection.

Virtual Colonoscopy

The **virtual colonoscopy** is a relative newcomer to imaging. Rather than undertaking an invasive probe inserted into the rectum, the patient is simply prepped and scanned with a CT machine. The images produced usually uncover abnormalities that merit follow-up with a traditional full colonoscopy procedure. However, without abnormalities present, the patient is spared undertaking the complete procedure.

Nuclear Medicine

Nuclear medicine is best defined as the diagnosis and treatment of many systems and parts of the body (including bones, heart and lungs, brain) through the use of minute amounts of radiopharmaceuticals (radioactive isotopes) that have been injected into the patient to produce a "real-time" image of the body, including organ functions and structure. The difference between nuclear medicine and other imaging procedures is that the images produced record the physiology (*function*) as well as anatomy (*structure*) of the organ or tissue of interest, which is necessary in the evaluation, diagnosis, and recommended treatment.

Positron Emission Tomography

Positron emission tomography (PET) is a useful procedure that creates three-dimensional images or maps of areas of interest to study a functional process. When available, PETs are often used in studies of brain functions.

Angiography/Interventional Radiology

Also known as an angiogram or arteriogram, **angiography** consists of x-rays and dye to view the inside of arteries in many parts of the body, including the heart, brain, and lungs. Contrast dye is injected into the blood and x-rays are taken to see if there are blocked or injured arteries. There are risks associated mainly with the contrast dye for patients who are allergic; blood clots and damage to blood vessels are other risks.

Electroencephalography

Electroencephalography (EEG) is a simple test to measure electrical brain activities, commonly used for epileptic studies or in cases of trauma to the head.

Electromyography

Electromyography (EMG) measures the electrical activity of muscles. It commonly is used in diagnosing nerve and muscle dysfunctions. A neurologist or physiatrist commonly uses an EMG machine in the diagnosis of their patients.

Electrocardiography

Electrocardiography (ECG) detects and records the electrical activity of the heart. It is more often found in a cardiac center and can involve the patient participating in a treadmill stress test.

CHAPTER SUMMARY

Outpatient imaging centers are common today and are growing in number. Patients are referred by their physicians and then imaged at the center. Later, after the radiologist reads the image and dictates his or her report, it is sent to the physician who uses it in the diagnosis of the patient's problem and to map a course of treatment.

CHAPTER REVIEW

1. How are CTs and MRIs different?
2. When would an EEG be ordered? An ECG? An EMG?
3. Why has there been a trend toward outpatient imaging centers and away from utilizing the hospital to produce most images? Is this a good thing or does it assist in making hospitals unprofitable?
4. Why would more patients likely opt for a virtual colonoscopy than the traditional method of performing a colonoscopy? Is the virtual colonoscopy as efficient at finding tumors as the traditional colonoscopy method?
5. Should physicians opt for an MRI rather than a normal x-ray due to the MRI not using radiation? What about spiraling healthcare costs?

Discussion: Should physicians be allowed to invest in outpatient imaging centers to where they send their patients? Will this result in over-utilization and is it prohibited under some of the federal healthcare laws?

Part III

Acute Care
Treatment Options
(presented alphabetically)

Chapter 8

The Allergy Clinic

<table>
<tr><td colspan="2" align="center">**Key Terms**</td></tr>
<tr><td>Allergies</td><td>Genetic predisposition</td></tr>
<tr><td>Asthma</td><td>Immunologist</td></tr>
</table>

INTRODUCTION

Few people escape having an allergy of one kind or another. Itchy, watery eyes or a runny nose from seasonal blooming flowers and trees; wheezing and coughing from triggering an asthmatic reaction; skin rashes from foods; and redness, swelling, and itching of the skin from insect bites may all signal some type of allergy. For those fortunate enough not to have chronic **allergies**, a visit to the family physician who can prescribe an antihistamine or decongestant is usually all that's required. For those not so lucky, a visit with an allergist/immunologist may be in order.

THE ALLERGIST/IMMUNOLOGIST

Because allergies are more often treated than prevented, they are most often controlled through allergen identification. An allergist/**immunologist** is a physician who is trained in the diagnosis and treatment of allergic diseases and **asthma** as well as other diseases of the immune system. The allergist usually attends 4 years of medical school followed by 3 years of residency in either internal medicine or pediatric medicine. An additional 2-year fellowship and an examination are required to become board certified in allergy and immunology.

Most people who seek an allergist/immunologist are referred by their primary care physician. They seek diagnosis and treatment for all allergic diseases such as those that trigger asthmatic reactions, allergic eye diseases, and chronic coughs and colds; in addition, testing may be performed to determine what allergen is causing the allergic reaction.

ALLERGY SYMPTOMS

An allergy is defined as an over-reaction to a usually harmless substance that the immune system determines is harmful, even if it is not. When the immune system is challenged with an allergen (the substance that causes an allergic reaction) it becomes sensitized, committing the allergen to memory. From that moment forward, the immune system recognizes the allergen and sets up a defense by releasing chemicals into the blood that may cause a runny nose, watery eyes, sneezing, or congestion.

Allergy symptoms are categorized as mild (affecting a precise area of the body), moderate (symptoms like itching that may spread to other parts of the body), and severe (also called anaphylaxis), which may affect the entire body and can be a life-threatening emergency.

COMMON ALLERGIES

- Hayfever: This is a common allergy occurring most often in the spring and summer months when pollen and mold spore counts are highest. Symptoms may include a runny nose, sneezing, and nasal obstruction. Medications to treat hayfever include corticosteroids, antihistamines, or decongestants in nasal sprays or oral tablets.
- Asthma: This disease affects the respiratory system and can cause repeated episodes of wheezing, breathlessness, tightness of chest, and coughing. If the asthma attack is severe, it can be quite disabling. Asthma can be controlled with medication and by recognizing the hazards that cause symptoms.
- Pet allergy: Probably the most common pet allergy is to cats. Small, invisible flakes of skin known as dander are the culprit in pet allergies, causing itching watery eyes, runny nose, and sneezing. The protein in pet saliva from dogs, cats, and horses can also cause allergies in some people but are usually less common. Urine from rabbits and hamsters can create an allergic reaction in some people. Antihistamines and decongestants may help to control the symptoms of pet allergies.
- Dust mite allergy: These microscopic organisms thrive in warm humid areas such as mattresses, carpet, and upholstery; they may create allergy

symptoms like wheezing, a runny nose, or watery eyes. Medications such as antihistamines and decongestants may be used in the treatment of dust mite allergies.

- Food allergy: A reaction to certain foods involves the immune system and can be life-threatening. Within minutes of consuming an offending food, the person will have symptoms such as tingling or swelling of the lips, tongue, or throat. Stomach pain, diarrhea, nausea and vomiting, along with dizziness or lightheadedness are often a result of food allergies. An extreme reaction can result in anaphylactic shock, which usually causes difficulties in breathing and possibly shock. Food allergies can best be avoided by rejecting the food responsible for the allergy. If a person experiences a food allergy despite that effort, a trip to the emergency room for an injection of epinephrine may be in order. Peanut allergy is the most common life-threatening allergic reaction that results in anaphylactic shock. People who are aware that they have a food allergy are cautioned to read food labels and to wear a medical alert bracelet that identifies the food allergy.

- Other allergies: Latex rubber (a problem for dental and healthcare workers who wear latex gloves), skin care products such as perfume and cosmetics, hair dyes, and poison ivy and other poisonous plants can also cause allergies. (These are discussed further in Chapter 11.)

DIAGNOSING ALLERGIES

As with any medical diagnosis, a thorough medical history is the foundation for detecting allergies. If several family members have or have had an allergic reaction, it is probably a safe bet that the patient, through **genetic predisposition**, could also be diagnosed with the same allergy.

A skin test may assist in the identification of the allergen that is causing the allergy symptoms. A simple skin prick with an allergen extract creates a positive reaction if the patient is allergic to that particular allergen. It is usually uncommon for a person to have an immediate allergic reaction, but tests should always be performed under the guidance of a doctor. Test results are usually available within a matter of minutes.

ALLERGEN IMMUNOTHERAPY TREATMENT

Once the diagnosis is confirmed and the correct cause of the allergy is established, the allergist/immunologist will decide the course of treatment. Of course, the best prevention is avoiding exposure to the allergen, but when that is not possible, treatments are available. Over-the-counter antihistamines, decongestants, and corticosteroids as well as prescription medications are available in pill form, liquid, nasal spray, inhaler (for asthma), or eye drops.

Allergies previously unknown rarely arrive quickly. An example could be an attack from hornets that results in an allergic reaction that necessitates treatment with an oral anti-inflammatory steroid.

For those people who suffer from severe allergies lasting more than 3 months, immunotherapy (allergy shots) could be the best course of treatment. By gradually increasing the offending allergen, the patient may build up immunity and become less sensitive to future exposure of the allergen.

CHAPTER SUMMARY

Many people suffer from allergies and allergic reactions. Specialists address these problems through their allergy clinics and practices. Assistance may be in the form of identification, education, prevention, and, when needed, treatment. A proactive step may be to desensitize the patient through immunotherapy, a series of timed medications designed to enhance immunity.

CHAPTER REVIEW

1. What are common forms of allergies?
2. What are some common allergy symptoms?
3. How does an allergy specialist diagnose allergies?
4. What are common treatment modalities for allergic reactions?
5. What is immunotherapy and how does it work?

Discussion: How can people with common allergies best cope with this challenge to their health? List three alternative methods.

Chapter 9

Chiropractic and Podiatry Care

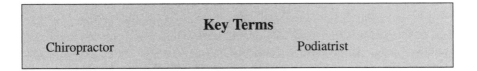

Key Terms	
Chiropractor	Podiatrist

INTRODUCTION

Chiropractic care is an alternative form of health care focusing on treating patients with drug-free, non-surgical, hands-on therapy called manipulation or adjustment. Podiatry care is a specialization that diagnoses and treats foot and ankle problems.

CHIROPRACTORS

It has taken about 100 years for chiropractic care to approach the point where it can be considered more in the mainstream of being a standard healthcare provider. As such, the issues surrounding the scope and role of chiropractic practices are receiving greater attention. Many important questions are now being asked: Is chiropractic care really an alternative to medicine? Some would argue that chiropractic care is not an alternative but is a viable addition to modern health care.

The word "chiropractic" combines the Greek words *cheir* (hand) and *praxis* (action) and means "done by hand." A **chiropractor** is a practitioner in the field of chiropractic care, an alternative healthcare profession that focuses on treating patients with drug-free, non-surgical, hands-on therapy called manipulation or adjustment. The central theme of chiropractic care lies in the relationship between the human body's structure, principally the musculoskeletal system and the nervous system, and its related disorders. The chiropractic approach to health care is

47

holistic, emphasizing the patient's complete health and well-being through examining many of the aspects that influence health, for example, diet, exercise, heredity, and the environment.

Health Problems Treated Through Chiropractic Care

Low-back pain is a major cause of functional disability representing one-fourth of all disabling work injuries (see http://bhpr.hrsa.gov/interdisciplinary/chiro.html). An estimated 80% of people can expect to experience an episode of low-back pain at some point in their lives. The direct and indirect costs of low-back pain are estimated at $60 billion annually in America (see http://bhpr.hrsa.gov/interdisciplinary/chiro.html).

Although most people visit a chiropractor for treatment of back pain or neck pain, other medical conditions may also be managed through chiropractic care. Pinched nerves (a nerve has been constricted or compressed causing numbness, tingling, and/or pain), tension headaches or migraines, or joint pain associated with arthritis are some problems that may be addressed by a chiropractor. Problems with coordination and balance can also sometimes be corrected with chiropractic care.

Injury Problems Treated Through Chiropractic Care

Injuries are also treated by means of chiropractic care. Among the most common are sports injuries that may result from a twist, rapid turn, or a fall from golf, baseball, basketball, soccer, and other sports. Automobile accidents often produce whiplash injuries to the neck and upper back, resulting from movements beyond the normal range of motion, sometimes resulting in soft tissue damage. These may respond to chiropractic care.

On-the-job injuries are seen quite commonly in chiropractic care, whether it be a pulled muscle, tendon, or carpal tunnel problems that result from repetitive motion. Stress relief is another reason many workers visit their local chiropractor. Many of these health problems and injuries may be treated with chiropractic care.

The Chiropractor's Office

A holistic approach to overall health, which can include diet and exercise, occupational and environmental study (both of the job and household), and approaches to stress, is often undertaken in the modern chiropractic office. The patient's medical history is taken upon arrival, along with any lifestyle information that may help in the treatment process. The method of payment is also important due to ever increasing changes in third-party reimbursement.

More health maintenance organizations and private health insurance companies are recognizing chiropractic care as a viable approach to health care; therefore, more are paying for chiropractic services. In addition, usually state workers' compensation plans, Medicare, and Medicaid pay for chiropractic treatment.

The chiropractor performs an examination to help detect the cause of the problem and makes a determination as to whether chiropractic care could help. If necessary, x-rays, computed tomography, magnetic resonance imaging, or laboratory testing is done to assist in making a diagnosis or to rule out certain conditions. The chiropractic practitioner then explains the diagnosis to the patient and recommends a treatment plan or discusses alternative forms of treatment. If chiropractic care is not the answer, the chiropractor will offer a referral to a medical physician, such as an orthopedic surgeon, neurologist, neurosurgeon, pain management specialist, or other appropriate caregivers.

Treatment Plans

Some chiropractors use spinal manipulation or adjustment techniques to enhance joint mobilization. Chiropractors may believe that subluxations (misalignments of the spine) interfere with the nervous system; this in turn may interfere with the body's natural healing ability. The focus is on correcting the subluxations through "adjustments" to the spinal vertebrae column. A chiropractic physician understands the role of each of the three areas of vertebrae—cervical, thoracic, and lumbar—and how he or she can assist the human body to restore balance in its own curative system. Examples of other plans in chiropractic care are soft tissue therapy, ultrasound or electrical stimulation, and therapeutic exercise, which includes flexibility and strength training.

The number of treatments depends on the type and severity of the condition, along with age and other health factors of the patient. Also taken into consideration is the length of time the condition has continued. Some patients enjoy relief in a short time; others may experience a more chronic condition. Some find that a visit to their chiropractor for manipulation/adjustment therapy even when there are no acute problems results in simply feeling better.

PODIATRISTS

Many Americans spend a lot of time on their feet, and a large percentage of the population experience foot problems. Enter the **podiatrist**, or the foot doctor. Doctors of Podiatric Medicine (DPMs) are specialists in diagnosing and treating foot and ankle problems. Podiatry was once called "chiropody," but that name, along with "chiropodist," is considered out of vogue in the United States, although both are still in used in the United Kingdom and much of the world. The terms are synonymous.

Podiatrists usually work in private practice and may specialize in different areas, including pediatric podiatry (podopediatrics) or geriatric podiatry (podogeriatrics). Podiatric physicians attend a 4-year podiatric medical school, followed by a residency for 2 to 3 years where they are trained in all major areas of clinical and surgical medicine.

Just as all medical doctors in the United States are licensed by the state in which they practice, so too are podiatrists who are state board certified in their specialty. As in most areas of health care, podiatry is a growing field, in part due to the increasingly aging population.

Reasons for Podiatry Care

Common foot problems like corns and calluses, bunions, ingrown toenails, and heel pain are all conditions that most of us will experience due to ill-fitting shoes, heredity, or simply as a part of the aging process. Physical therapy is often used to treat those problems and may include massage, diathermy (electrically induced heat), or perhaps hot packs. Surgery is sometimes performed to correct a bunion problem and remove cysts or tumors. Podiatrists encourage patients to wear shoes and socks that fit properly and comfortably to alleviate many foot aggravations.

High-impact sports activities played on artificial surfaces, like football, basketball, and soccer, often contribute to foot and ankle injuries. Examples are:

* Ankle sprains
* Heel pain
* Runner's knee
* "Turf toe" (result of the big toe being hyperextended)

Dancers (especially ballet) often experience foot, ankle, and lower leg stresses that require podiatric care.

Arthritis in the feet or ankles is a disease involving the joints and can be treated with anti-inflammatory medications, physical therapy, and, sometimes, orthoses (shoes that have been prescribed specifically for the patient). Podiatrists use x-rays, laboratory tests, and, at times, computed tomography to help diagnose foot and ankle diseases like arthritis and tumors and to determine the course of treatment. If the course of treatment is beyond the scope of the podiatrist, often the patient is referred to an orthopedic surgeon.

Being overweight is another risk factor that can make a person more vulnerable to stress on the bones of the feet as well as turning the ankle. Being overweight can also contribute to diabetes, another disease that exacerbates foot problems through infections and foot ulcers caused by poor circulation.

CHAPTER SUMMARY

Chiropractors are practitioners who specialize in the manipulation of the skeletal and muscular systems. They may offer relief of occupational injuries or automobile whiplash-induced problems or from pinched nerves. Most take a holistic approach in treating patients and may refer many to other types of practitioners.

Podiatrists are practitioners who specialize in the care of feet and foot injuries. They may offer advice in preventing injuries, assist with nail grooming and the removal of painful and unwanted growths, and many specialize in treating athletes with sports injuries.

CHAPTER REVIEW

1. What are some injuries for which chiropractic care may be successfully applied?
2. What treatments do chiropractors offer?
3. What are likely injuries that a podiatrist may treat?
4. If a patient visits a chiropractor and is seen to be beyond the scope of chiropractic care, what should the chiropractor do with the patient?
5. If a patient is seen by a podiatrist and is beyond the care of the podiatrist, to whom is the podiatrist likely to refer him or her?

Discussion: Your friend was driving yesterday and another vehicle ran into the back of your friend's vehicle. Your friend has sought your advice regarding neck pains he is experiencing. What treatment options do you suggest?

Chapter 10

Dentistry

Key Terms

Dental assistant	Orthodontist
Dental hygienist	Pediatric dentistry
Dental laboratory technician	Periodontitis
Dentist	Prosthodontist
Endodontist	

INTRODUCTION

Going to the dentist is probably not on the "Top Ten List of Most Favorite Things to Do" for most people. As much as we dread sitting in that dental chair, however, we are convinced that good oral health is an indication of good overall health. Public health measures, such as fluoridation of drinking water and consumer education on proper dental hygiene, have helped bring about a decline in cavities in the past 50 years. Today, half of all American children under 12 have never had a cavity. For adults, these preventive measures, along with new filling materials, are enabling many of us to keep our own teeth for the rest of our lives. Strong teeth and gums are essential for one to chew the right food that contributes to good health, and that's where a dentist comes in.

GENERAL DENTISTRY

A **dentist** is a licensed doctor who has graduated from an accredited dental school, usually a 4-year experience after 4 years of college. A Doctor of Dental Surgery (DDS) or Doctor of Dental Medicine (DDM) is the degree awarded in dentistry. Some doctors choose to train in specialty areas of dentistry such as oral surgery, orthodontics, or pediatric dentistry. Each of these is discussed later. Every state issues a license for the dentist to practice on a state-by-state basis as either a solo practitioner or in a dental partnership, with a few dentists working in hospitals.

An assortment of equipment can be found in the dental office, including x-ray machines, drills, cuspidor (sink), overhead lights, reclining patient chair, and carts for holding dental supplies. The more technologically advanced offices offer procedures with dental laser that promise "no drill, no needles, pain free" dentistry.

Depending on the size of the practice, employees may include a receptionist who usually processes appointments, an office manager, a billing/insurance specialist, dental hygienists, dental assistants, and, of course, the dentist, who typically is responsible for training and supervising his staff.

THE DENTIST'S ROLE

The dentist checks all teeth and the gums. He or she studies x-rays for potential problems like decay, checks the patient's bite to see that the top and bottom teeth work together, examines the mouth for other problems like oral cancer, and provides information regarding tooth, gum, and mouth care to the patient to prevent future problems. (Oral cancer is a severe disease of the mouth, lips, and throat and can be detected through regular dental checkups. It is more treatable if spotted early, which makes regular dental visits all the more important.) If decay is present, the dentist advises the patient to schedule a future appointment for filling the cavities. Other procedures, such as tooth extraction, root canals, and gum disease, are usually addressed in subsequent appointments providing there is no emergency.

DENTAL HYGIENIST

Before seeing the dentist, a **dental hygienist** meets with the patient and determines the reason for the visit. She or he updates the medical and dental history and then begins an examination of the mouth while screening the patient for oral cancer. The dental hygienist also may clean and polish the teeth, thereby removing plaque, and follow this by brushing and flossing the teeth and the spaces between the teeth. Tobacco, tea, and coffee stains are removed for an enhanced appearance. If required, x-rays are taken to discover if there are cavities. A fluoride treatment to prevent future cavities may follow. A dental hygienist also takes measurements and prepares impressions for dentures or partials to replace missing teeth.

In some states, hygienists are allowed to administer anesthetics but are not allowed to diagnose diseases. Sometimes they work alongside the dentist during treatment.

Dental hygienists have to be licensed in the state where they work, just as a dentist does, after having graduated from an accredited dental hygiene school and passing both a written and clinical examination. Because schedules are flexible for most dental hygienists, some may work in more than one dental office, working 2 or 3 days a week in each.

DENTAL ASSISTANT

Unlike dental hygienists, the **dental assistant** usually trains on the job, whereas some attend dental-assisting programs, usually at a local community or junior college for 1 year or less. The U.S. military, technical institutes, and trade schools are other sources for learning dental assisting.

Dental assistants carry out duties with more emphasis on patient services and office and laboratory duties, as opposed to dental hygienists, who perform more clinical tasks. Typical tasks performed by dental assistants are to:

- Prepare patients for dental procedures
- Assist by handing instruments and materials to the dentist
- Prepare trays of instruments
- Maintain infection control according to Occupational Safety and Health Administration regulations
- Prepare materials for impressions and restorations
- Take dental x-rays
- Instruct patients in postoperative care

Dental assistants are regulated on a state-by-state basis with some requiring licensure, registration, or certification. Some states require assistants to pass a written or "practical" examination to be licensed or registered, whereas other states call for little or no education. Dental assistants who perform advanced duties like radiological procedures must satisfactorily complete a state-approved course.

Dental assisting can be an entry-level job for someone wanting to move up in dentistry. The assistant can return to school for a dental hygienist degree, move into dental sales or dental office management, or become dental-assisting instructors.

DENTAL LABORATORY TECHNICIAN

Dental prosthetics, including bridges and crowns, are constructed by the **dental laboratory technician** based on impressions and specifications sent by the dentist after a patient has had an impression made of the mouth and/or teeth in the dentist's office. Through a series of steps, a patient can be fitted with an almost exact replica of his or her lost tooth or teeth. Dental laboratory technicians work with dentists in the manufacture of complete or partial dentures and with orthodontists in making orthodontic appliances like braces and retainers.

DENTAL SPECIALISTS

Pediatric Dentist

A pediatric dentist specializes in the dental treatment of children only, unlike a general dentist who treats adults as well as children. This specialist has completed 4 years of dental school with an additional 2 to 3 years specializing in the oral health of children. The focus on children is to teach good dental habits at an early age through prevention. Early detection prevents dental disease as they age. As in a general dentist's office, the pediatric dental staff comprises the dentist, dental hygienist, dental assistant, and office personnel who are all trained in the importance of **pediatric dentistry**.

Orthodontist

An **orthodontist** is a dentist who, after dental school, must successfully complete another 2- to 3-year accredited residency program in orthodontics, the area of dentistry that specializes in diagnosing, treating, and preventing dental irregularities.

Braces are not just for children anymore. Many adults are fitted with braces that are worn for 2 to 3 years, depending on age, how well the treatment plan is followed, and the desired outcome as set forth by the orthodontist and the patient. Most likely, a patient is referred to the orthodontist by the patient's dentist for treatment of a malocclusion (misaligned teeth) through braces or other procedures. In addition to straightening teeth, braces can correct overbites, underbites, or correct jaw alignment.

Periodontist

A periodontist is a dentist who specializes in diagnosing, treating, and preventing diseases of the gums and bones around the teeth. Periodontists must complete 4 years of dental school followed by 3 years of specialty training.

Periodontal disease (**periodontitis**) is a severe, chronic gum disease that causes bone loss and is permanent. Affected teeth are often lost to the disease, resulting in the person having to wear dentures or having tooth implants. Periodontitis is the late stage of gingivitis that has been left untreated. Other factors that may affect the gums and cause the disease are smoking or tobacco use of any kind, genetics, stress that causes clenching or grinding of the teeth (especially during sleep), some medications, diabetes, and pregnancy. A poor diet can worsen already diseased gums. Periodontitis, if left untreated, can increase the risk of heart attacks or strokes.

Periodontitis can be corrected at an early stage with removing plaque around the teeth by scaling. At a later stage, treatment is usually with periodontal surgery when the periodontist determines that the gums cannot be cared for with non-surgical treatment. Soft tissue grafts may be performed to replace damaged tissue or dental implants may be the recommended course of action if a tooth has already been lost due to periodontal disease.

Endodontist

The **endodontist** specializes in root canal therapy. Like other dental specialists, endodontists must graduate from a 4-year dental school and then complete 2 or more years of specialty training. Endodontists attempt to save teeth based on root canal therapy, which necessitates the removal of the dental pulp when it has become inflamed or infected and cannot be successfully treated. The procedure is normally done in one or two visits.

Oral and Maxillofacial Surgeon

Oral and maxillofacial surgeons are dental specialists who treat and diagnose injuries, defects, and diseases of the mouth, gums, jaw, neck, teeth, and face. They are 4-year graduates from a dental school that have trained for a minimum of 4 years in a hospital surgical residency. Victims of facial trauma sustained in an accident are often provided reconstructive surgery by an oral surgeon. Patients with cancer of the maxillofacial areas are cared for by an oral surgeon who usually also has advanced training in pain control, providing the patient with better comfort.

Cosmetic Dentistry

With a worldwide focus on looking younger and better, cosmetic dentistry is another way to achieve an enhanced appearance. Cosmetic dentistry focuses on improving the appearance of one's teeth, mouth, and smile through dentistry procedures that can include:

- Teeth whitening through bleaching
- Reshaping teeth to match the others
- Filling cavities or repairing chipped teeth with composite resin bonding to match the patient's other teeth

- Porcelain or plastic veneers to cover broken teeth or imperfections
- Dental implants to replace teeth that are lost due to
  - Growing older
  - Oral trauma
  - Poor oral hygiene

Most dental insurance plans do not cover cosmetic dental procedures, and the cost may vary from dentist to dentist. Virtually all dentists offer some type of cosmetic dentistry. Because of consumer demand, many dentists are now focusing their entire practice on cosmetic dentistry.

Prosthodontist

A **prosthodontist** is a specialist in the restoring of oral function through prostheses and restorations including dentures, crowns, and dental implants. Cosmetic dentistry can fall within the discipline of prosthodontics. Prosthodontists require an additional 3 years of specialty training after having completed dental college. They often deal with intricate dental problems of the entire mouth that may be caused by congenital defects or trauma. They also treat temporomandibular joint disorders and sleep apnea by constructing specialized prostheses or orthotic appliances.

CHAPTER SUMMARY

As with all areas of health care, the demand for dental care will grow with the aging population. Improved methods and new technology already allow people to keep their teeth at a later age than previous generations, though sometimes necessitating more trips to the dental office.

CHAPTER REVIEW

1. What is the difference between a dental assistant and a dental hygienist?
2. Who would you make an appointment with if you found your gums to be frequently bleeding?
3. Who would you make an appointment with to have your 5-year-old child's teeth examined?
4. Your 60-year-old grandmother has never taken care of her teeth and many have been pulled. Who should she now begin to make appointments with?

5. You have noticed that you awaken each morning with a sore jaw and suspect that you are clenching your teeth at night. Who should you make an appointment with?

Discussion: Medical science may be on the verge of discovering a mouthwash to kill bacteria that cause tooth decay. Do you believe this is a panacea that blackens the outlook for people contemplating dental careers?

Chapter 11

Dermatology

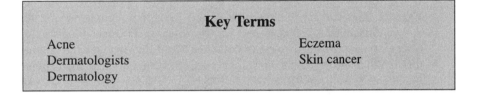

Key Terms

Acne
Dermatologists
Dermatology

Eczema
Skin cancer

INTRODUCTION

Dermatology is the branch of medicine that is relative to the diagnosis and treatment of problems to the skin, hair, and nails. The skin is the largest organ in the human body; skin cells produce hair and nails. All these are the first barrier to help to protect people from viruses and bacteria. Healthy skin, hair, and nails are important to maintain generally good health. When problematic conditions arise with any skin area, it may be wise to consult a dermatologist.

DERMATOLOGISTS

Dermatologists are medical doctors who specialize in medical, surgical, and cosmetic care for skin, hair, and nail conditions. After completing 4 years of medical school, every potential dermatologist receives 5 years of additional training, including a 2-year residency in dermatology. Dermatologists are the foremost specialists in all aspects of skin, including the prevention of skin diseases, skin cancers, and cosmetic skin care. They generally work in private practice but may also be found in managed care (e.g., health maintenance organizations), hospitals, or academic medicine.

COMMON SKIN DISEASES

- **Acne:** One of the most common skin disorders, acne was previously believed to be caused by poor hygiene, poor diet (including drinking too many soft drinks and eating greasy foods), or the overall stress of being a teenager. In actuality, it is a skin condition that happens when oil, bacteria, and skin cells clog a hair follicle. Acne is not unique to teens; adults have it as well. Clogged pores become eruptions on the skin called "pimples," which can appear on the face, neck, and back. After examination and diagnosis, a dermatologist designs a treatment program using a combination of topical medications (creams or gels to kill bacteria), oral medications (e.g., antibiotics), and/or more specialized therapy such as liquid nitrogen spray for inflammation or steroids that are used to treat difficult lesions.

- **Eczema:** This skin condition crosses all ages but is most common in infants and young adults. There is no cure for this disease, but dermatologists can offer treatments that help to control eczema. Moisturizing soaps and oils aid the skin in maintaining the moisture needed to prevent dryness and itching. Ointments and creams prescribed by a dermatologist may also offer success in managing an itch. Simple measures such as using a gentle laundry detergent and avoiding products that contain fragrances may aid in management.

- **Skin cancer:** Basal cell carcinoma, squamous cell carcinoma, and melanoma are three of the most common skin cancers. Long-term exposure to the sun, internal illnesses, and genetics may link a person to skin cancer. Skin cancers that are confined to the dermis (skin) can be treated by a dermatologist with excision. The best methods for prevention of skin cancers are commonly thought to be sun protection at an early age through the use of sunscreens (creams or lotions to block dangerous ultraviolet A and B rays), regular self-skin examinations, and annual visits to a dermatologist.

INDUSTRIAL DERMATOLOGY

Certain occupations are more prone to exposure of chemicals and substances that can cause allergic contact dermatitis:

- Dental and healthcare workers may experience work-related contact dermatitis by using latex gloves and by continuously washing their hands with soaps that may dry the skin.

- Wholesale florists and market gardeners who handle plants such as chrysanthemums and tulips can experience dermatitis due to the allergens in the flowers.

- Laundry workers and housekeepers may be exposed to many allergens in soaps, cleaners, chemicals, and waxes.
- Hairdressers are at risk of developing chronic hand or eyelid dermatitis as a result of chemicals in hair products such as dyes, shampoos, aerosols, and bleaches.
- Machinists use cutting oils, fluids, and petroleum-based solvents that may cause contact dermatitis.

Prevention, of course, is the key to reducing occupational exposures that may result in skin disease. Management and workers must commit to learning about and implementing proper prevention procedures such as barrier creams. Personal safety equipment in the form of gloves, safety glasses, aprons, and shop coats should be available to all workers to control their exposure to irritants and allergens that cause problematic skin conditions. Instead of attempting to treat a skin disorder with over-the-counter medications, workers should be encouraged to seek dermatological help in identifying, controlling, or eliminating the skin disease altogether.

COSMETIC DERMATOLOGY

With an enormous focus on youth, beauty, and appearance, people around the globe are turning to their dermatologists to correct skin imperfections. Not only are those who are in the limelight turning to cosmetic corrections, many in the business world who want to look youthful and relaxed are also visiting dermatologists.

One approach to looking younger is a simple in-office treatment completed in a matter of minutes. Injections of a highly diluted form of botulinum toxin A (i.e., botox) assist in reducing wrinkles and signs of aging. Frown and/or laugh lines seemingly disappear as do crow's feet and forehead creases. This may be a good solution for people who want to look stress-free and rested without having to undergo cosmetic surgery.

Other cosmetic dermatology procedures are as follows:

- Birthmark removal: Birthmarks come in all sizes, colors, and shapes with unique names for each. Former Soviet leader Mikhail Gorbachev had a sizable port wine stain on his forehead but did not seem daunted by its presence. Others, however, may be more sensitive. A usually safe and effective laser treatment by a dermatologist can remove a birthmark.
- Tattoo removal: Along the same lines as birthmarks, these identifiers have been "self-inflicted." Some consider their tattoo a youthful folly that no longer fits their lifestyle or perhaps an unwanted reminder of someone from

the past. They then may wish to have it removed with a laser treatment by a dermatologist.

- Hair removal: A laser treatment is also used to remove unwanted hair on all parts of the body. The most common areas for hair removal are usually the upper lip, ears and nose, the bikini line, neck, chest, arms, and legs.
- Hair restoration: Although others may have too much hair in what they consider to be inappropriate places, some suffer balding and hair loss. Both men and women experience this condition due to age, illness, and/or heredity. One's own hair can be removed from areas where there is a lot of it and then surgically implanted in the balding area. The hair then grows normally, giving a complete, natural look. Treatments are performed in several sessions by an experienced dermatologist.
- Aging skin: As we age, our skin usually becomes thinner and more fragile. With that may come age spots, or "liver spots," which really have nothing to do with the liver except perhaps the perceived color. Caused by years of exposure to the sun, sun spots may be reduced or lightened with "fade" creams or laser therapy.

Cosmetic dermatology now holds many new, exciting options for correcting what Mother Nature did not give us at birth. People can, however, implement protective measures to ensure healthy skin:

- Staying out of the sun
- Wearing sunscreen
- Not engaging in artificial tanning
- Self-checking their skin frequently
- Visiting a dermatologist annually

CHAPTER SUMMARY

There are many individuals who seek dermatologists on a regular basis. This may include golfers with small skin cancers, teens with skin eruptions, seniors who wish to appear younger, or those working in occupations that encounter chemical exposures. The practice of dermatology can address many of these issues.

CHAPTER REVIEW

1. What are some methods that dermatologists use to remove tattoos and birthmarks?

2. What are common problems that may cause individuals to need the care of a dermatologist?
3. How can individuals help to preserve their skin and not encounter skin-related problems?
4. The Occupational Safety and Health Administration guarantees to every American worker a safe and healthy workplace. What is management required to do to protect workers from dermatitis-related health problems?
5. Illustrate ways that you believe a dermatologist can act to prevent skin-related problems among his or her patients.

Discussion: Should tanning salons be better regulated to decrease harmful exposure, or should consumers become better educated as to potential health problems that may be caused by tanning salons?

Chapter 12

Hearing and Speaking: Audiology and Speech Pathology

Key Terms	
Audiologist	Speech pathologist

INTRODUCTION

An **audiologist** assists patients that experience hearing loss and hearing-related problems, whereas a **speech pathologist** works with patients who have reduced ability to communicate by speaking.

AUDIOLOGY

Audiologists commonly work with those who have hearing, ear, or balance-related ear problems. They perform hearing tests, identifying those with temporary hearing loss or permanent hearing loss, measuring the extent of the problem, and then assisting the patient however possible.

Using audiometers in soundproof booths, they measure the loudness and frequencies at which the patient hears and record the hearing loss and in what frequency ranges it occurs. They then interview the patient about the likely causes and impacts of the loss on the person's life.

Audiologists may also work with companies to measure the baseline of hearing during the employment process, thus helping management to document whether the person experienced hearing loss over the course of his or her employment and what might have caused the loss. In addition, audiologists may use specialized equipment to evaluate and diagnose balance disorders.

Hearing disorders may result from causes such as birth trauma, preexisting genetic disorders, viral infections, exposure to loud noise, medications of certain types, or normal aging. Treatments may include simply cleaning the ear canal and fitting and dispensing hearing aids. Audiology treatments may also include counseling and adjusting to the loss of hearing, training to use hearing aid instruments, and teaching strategies of communication for use in a host of environments, such as on the job, at home, or during recreation.

Audiologists may work in schools, own their own office, and accept referrals from physicians, physical therapists, or occupational therapists. Some audiologists specialize in treatment of the elderly; others specialize in treatment of children. Yet others specialize in the workplace, measuring workplace noise and then developing strategies to protect workers from hearing loss. Audiologists may be a wonderful source for patients to learn about signing as a method of communication.

SPEECH PATHOLOGY

Speech pathologists diagnose and treat speech and language disorders and evaluate oral mechanisms that are responsible for eating and swallowing. Patients may require speech and language services after a stroke, surgery, head injury, or cancer of the neck and head. Speech problems can be (1) congenital, such as a cleft palate or mental retardation; (2) developmental, such as stuttering; (3) acquired through injury; or (4) from chronic diseases, such as Parkinson's disease.

Patients should be seen by the speech pathologist as quickly as possible after the communication disorder is identified. Often, the medical treatment and speech therapy may be concurrent. The goal of the speech therapist is to maximize the most functional communication possible. This can be on an inpatient or outpatient basis.

Speech pathologists may also work with patients who have speech fluency and rhythm problems, such as stuttering, and people with voice disorders, perhaps caused by a hearing impairment from an early age. They may also assist those who might want to improve communications skills by learning or modifying an accent, such as an actor wishing to portray a foreign character.

For those with little or no capability for speech, the pathologist may select an alternative method of communication. This may be an automatic device such as a portable keyboard device or sign language. Speech pathologists may also help patients develop compensatory strategies in order to swallow without choking or inhaling foods or liquids.

CHAPTER SUMMARY

Audiologists assist patients who experience hearing loss and hearing-related problems. They may also assist patients with balancing problems. Audiologists may be retained by management to establish hearing baselines for new employees and to develop strategies to prevent hearing loss among workers. Audiologists may suggest hearing aids or other communication devices to assist those who are hearing impaired.

Speech pathologists work with patients who have reduced ability to communicate by speaking, for example, stroke patients, cancer patients, and patients with congenital speech problems or injuries. They may also assist patients with stuttering problems or issues with swallowing.

CHAPTER REVIEW

1. What type of patient might an audiologist treat?
2. What are some techniques that an audiologist might use to help a hearing challenged patient?
3. How might management use an audiologist in a large manufacturing facility?
4. Who are various types of patients that might be seen at a speech therapy clinic?
5. What are some suggested methods to improve communications for those who are challenged with speaking problems?

Discussion: Congress has passed strong laws under the Americans with Disabilities Act (ADA), protecting citizens with limitations of everyday living. Discuss management's duty to accommodate workers who are challenged with hearing and speaking limitations.

Chapter 13

In Vitro Fertilization as a Form of Assisted Reproductive Technology

<table>
<tr><td colspan="2" align="center">Key Terms</td></tr>
<tr><td>Assisted reproductive technology (ART)</td><td>In vitro fertilization (IVF)</td></tr>
<tr><td>Bioethics</td><td>In vivo fertilization</td></tr>
<tr><td>Embryo</td><td>Zygote intrafallopian</td></tr>
<tr><td>Gamete intrafallopian transfer (GIFT)</td><td> transfer (ZIFT)</td></tr>
</table>

INTRODUCTION

In vitro fertilization (IVF) is the joining of a man's sperm and a woman's egg outside the womb in a laboratory dish, test tube, or beaker. "In vitro" means outside of the body, and fertilization happens when the sperm has entered the egg.

IVF is one form of **assisted reproductive technology (ART)**. There are many forms of ART; techniques have been successfully used since 1978 with the birth of Baby Brown in England, followed by successful births in India, Australia, and in the United States in 1981.

THE MOST COMMON PROCEDURE

Couples having problems conceiving children may wish to employ a widely used approach in which the technique is commonly conducted in the following sequence (see http://www.nlm.nih.gov/medlineplus/ency/article/007279.htm):

1. Superovulation stimulation is performed to boost egg production, which may result in the production of several eggs each month.
2. Retrieval of the eggs, called follicular aspiration, is undertaken. The woman is first given pain-reducing medicines in an outpatient setting, usually

a physician's office. Using ultrasound to find the eggs, a technician inserts a needle through the vagina, into the ovary containing the eggs, and removes the eggs by aspiration or suction. If the woman is not producing eggs, a donor may be sought from which to request or to purchase eggs.

3. Sperm from the father-to-be or from a donor is then mixed with what are thought to be the best quality eggs. As an alternative, the IVF laboratory technician may directly inject sperm into the egg with a very fine needle.

4. After fertilization, the egg should begin to divide and thus become an **embryo**. The IVF technical staff monitors this to ensure all is proceeding normally. If there is a high risk of a heredity disorder, the embryo may be tested 3 to 4 days after fertilization by removing one cell and then screening it for the specific genetic disorder. The potential parents may then decide which embryo or embryos to implant in the mother-to-be.

5. The couple and physician decide which and how many embryos to implant, a decision known as embryo transfer; this is often driven by the woman's age. During the transfer procedure, the physician inserts a catheter containing the embryos into the vagina and up into the womb. If the embryo sticks to the lining and grows, pregnancy results. Remaining embryos may be frozen and implanted at a later date, or the remaining embryos may be donated to other waiting couples.

6. After the embryo transfer, the mother-to-be takes daily shots or pills of progesterone for 8 to 10 weeks; this is a hormone to thicken the uterus lining, making the embryo easier to successfully implant. Too little progesterone can result in a miscarriage.

7. About 12 to 14 days after the transfer, a pregnancy test is conducted.

COST OF THE PROCEDURE

Often, insurance companies do not cover the cost of the procedure. This can be an expensive undertaking when one considers the costs of the clinic, physician, anesthesia, ultrasounds, surgery, blood tests, processing the sperm and eggs, storage of the embryo, and transfer of the embryo. In early 2008 this could cost in the range of $18,000 to $24,000 per IVF cycle.

RISKS AND ADVANTAGES

The chief risk of IVF is multiple births. Several embryos are implanted to ensure success, and in many instances all attach to the uterus successfully. If multiple embryos are generated, many patients choose to freeze those that are not transferred. Thus if the conception fails, the patient may harvest a frozen embryo to again implant, thus avoiding the expense and trouble of a complete IVF cycle. As an added benefit, if a pregnancy occurs and is carried to term, the patient can always then choose to become pregnant again at a later time using one of the remaining embryos.

OTHER ART FORMS

There are other ART forms, but detailed discussion of these is beyond the scope of this text. However, two are worth mentioning here:

- **Gamete intrafallopian transfer**: Unfertilized eggs and sperm are each transferred into the woman's fallopian tubes by use of a laparoscope through small incisions in the potential mother's abdomen. This allows **in vivo fertilization** rather than in vitro fertilization.
- **Zygote intrafallopian transfer**: Fertilized eggs are transferred into the woman's fallopian tubes, rather than the uterus, through use of a laparoscope.

BIOETHICS

Regarding **bioethics**, there is controversy in performing IVF and ART:

- Excess embryos are fertilized, which may result in eliminating some of the embryos.
- IVF procedures are not affordable to less affluent people.
- Embryos could be used unethically, such as implanting only those embryos containing genes dominant for blue eyes or tall stature, those that are male or female, or a host of other social reasons, rather than for reasons of health or genetic disease elimination.
- Embryos could be created solely for medical or research purposes.
- Embryos produced in this manner could be viewed as a commodity to be commercially exchanged, bought, or sold.

CHAPTER SUMMARY

ART may take several forms, and the most common is IVF. Though commonplace today, the techniques used are not always successful but are always expensive. There are many bioethical issues surrounding these techniques.

CHAPTER REVIEW

1. What are several methods of ART?
2. List the usual steps in performing an IVF procedure.

3. What are some of the bioethical issues regarding ART?
4. Regarding non-clinical and non-medical personnel, who are likely participants in an IVF procedure?
5. What are some of the risks and some of the advantages in an IVF procedure?

Discussion: Your friend is contemplating becoming a paid egg donor. What issues would you suggest she consider?

Chapter 14

Optometry, Dispensing Optometrists, and Ophthalmology . . . or, "The Eyes Have It"

INTRODUCTION

Eye care has come a long way in recent years, with new innovative techniques providing options for many patients who wear eyeglasses and/or contact lenses. In this chapter we discuss these options and define the various trained professionals in this field.

OPTOMETRISTS

An **optometrist**, or Doctor of Optometry (OD), provides most of what is known as "vision care." The optometrist usually examines a patient's eyes to determine visual acuity, color and depth perception, the ability to coordinate and focus the eyes, and any other eye problems or eye diseases. Optometrists may also administer drugs in the diagnosis of vision problems and prescribe drugs to treat some eye diseases.

Optometrists may provide pre- and postoperative care during laser correction procedures, cataract procedures, or for other eye surgery patients. They may diagnose conditions caused by high blood pressure, diabetes, or other chronic and systemic diseases. The limitations of an optometrist to diagnose and treat patients may vary by statute from state to state.

Optometrists should also not be confused with ophthalmologists or dispensing opticians, who are found in opposite spectrums of eye care. Ophthalmologists and dispensing opticians are discussed later in the chapter.

Most optometrists are in general practice, but some may specialize in children, the elderly, or those with partial sight. Some specialize in contact lenses, vision therapy, or helping those actively engaged in sports with their special vision needs. Many opticians purchase or operate franchise stores with the added advantage of brand identification and co-op advertising.

DISPENSING OPTICIANS

A **dispensing optician** is one who fits eyeglasses or contact lenses. Only about 20 states require a license, and most working in this field receive on-the-job training. When a patient enters the business or office of a dispensing optician, his or her prescription is examined to correctly determine the specifications of lenses. The dispensing optician then recommends eyeglass frames, lenses, and possibly lens coatings, after careful interviewing and considering the patient's work conditions, lifestyle, and facial features.

The dispensing optician usually measures the patient's face and physical features of the patient's eyes, noting the distance between the center of the pupils and the distance between the ocular surface and the proposed lens of the eyeglasses. He or she may also want to review the records from previous visits and, at the request of the patient, simply make new glasses in the same style as the patient's former glasses.

The dispensing optician sends a work order to an ophthalmic laboratory, giving information needed to grind and insert lenses into an eyeglass frame, the information containing color, style, material, and size of lens. The eyeglasses then return, ready for the frame to be fitted to the customer's face. After bending and reshaping the frame for a near-perfect fit, the customer or patient is instructed on issues of wearing and caring for the new glasses.

Dispensing opticians may also measure the shape and size of the patient's eyes to properly fit them for contact lenses. The customer or patient is observed as to eyes and eyelids, cornea, and other personal variables and then in follow-up visits given special instructions as to proper insertion, removal, care, and cleaning of the new contact lenses.

OPHTHALMOLOGISTS

An **ophthalmologist** attends 4 years of college, 4 years of medical school, a year of internship, and at least 3 years of residency in the diagnosis and medical-surgical treatment of disorders of the eye. Some ophthalmologists specialize in areas of eye care, such as pediatric eye problems, whereas others may specialize in surgery and undertake only cataract surgery. Still others may specialize in diseases such as glaucoma or in a particular section of the eye such as the retina. Some of these physicians treat eye diseases with medication. Other ophthalmologists may specialize in correcting abnormalities of vision or diseases that may require laser surgery or actual invasive surgery.

As a word of caution, an ophthalmologist is referred to as an "eye MD" by the American Academy of Ophthalmology. This can reduce confusion from other physicians such as an OD (Doctor of Optometry), who is usually called an optometrist, and a DO, who is a Doctor of Osteopathic Medicine, a physician similar to an MD (see Chapter 2).

ADVANCES IN EYE CARE

Great advances have been made in the field of eye care. One of these is **LASIK surgery**, which is a reshaping of the eye with the purpose of improving vision without the use of eyeglasses. Usually, a patient is given a careful examination. If the patient is found to be a suitable candidate, he or she are scheduled to have his or her eyes "mapped," giving the physician a suitable guide to use during the procedure.

Upon arriving for the LASIK procedure, the patient is given a mild sedative to help the patient to relax; after a few minutes the patient is ushered into the procedure room. The patient may be asked to recline on a table or in a dental-type chair. Numbing drops are placed in the patient's eye or eyes, and then the eye is reshaped with the help of the laser instrument. Normally, the actual procedure only takes a few seconds for each eye. Immediately, the patient may experience 20/20 or even better vision. A disadvantage of the procedure, however, is that although the patient may be able to discard his or her glasses for distant vision, older patients may need to acquire simple reading glasses to see print and near objects.

The U.S. Army is so convinced of the LASIK surgery procedure and the subsequent benefit of discontinuing glasses in young soldiers that "20/10 by 2010" has become a common slogan. This means the U.S. Army would like soldiers using glasses to have LASIK surgery in the hope of discarding their glasses; thus all soldiers possible could have 20/10 vision (the ability to see at 20 feet what normal people would have to get to 10 feet to see) by the year 2010.

Still another advance in the treatment of problems within the eye is that of cataract surgery. Cataracts are a simple clouding of the lens, usually as a result of aging or of trauma to the eye, causing the patient to experience their vision as though they are peering out of a foggy windshield. During the past 50 years cataract surgery was an ordeal, and lens replacement might cause the patient to be bedridden for days because of a large surgical incision made in each eye. Today, incisions are tiny (as small as 2 mm), and the patient might return to work the very next day. During the procedure a small ultrasound probe breaks the lens and another device sucks it out of the eye. The replacement lens, usually made from silicone, is rolled up and injected through the narrow slit and then unfolded, going naturally into place.

CHAPTER SUMMARY

Eye care has come a long way in recent years. For most patients, eyeglasses and contact lenses are no longer the only options to improve vision. Through the use of LASIK surgery, a person may experience perfect vision in a short period, perhaps in one visit for an examination and mapping and a second visit for the procedure.

Ophthalmologists are medical doctors trained in treating diseases of the eye. Optometrists are trained in examining patients for glasses and contact lenses. Dispensing opticians are those who measure and fit eyeglasses correctly to the patient's unique and individual features.

CHAPTER REVIEW

1. What are some advantages and disadvantages of glasses over contact lenses?
2. What are advantages and disadvantages of LASIK surgery over glasses and contact lenses?
3. What are the differences in the practice of an ophthalmologist and that of an optometrist?
4. What does a dispensing optician do?
5. Why should everyone have an annual eye examination?

Discussion: If you decide to have your eyes examined, do you believe should you visit an ophthalmologist or an optometrist? Why?

Chapter 15

Outpatient Surgery Centers

INTRODUCTION

We learned in Chapter 7 that physicians find it profitable to open imaging centers; this is also true of outpatient surgery centers (also sometimes known as outpatient surgicenters). Once nearly the exclusive domain of hospitals, surgery is now commonly performed on an outpatient basis, provided the patient may be safely discharged on the same day and does not have to reside overnight. Even this factor is no longer a barrier in some regions of the United States. Some physicians have taken the extra steps to provide staff, equipment, and beds to allow patients to stay safely overnight in the outpatient surgery center, thus becoming an overnight mini-hospital.

OUTPATIENT SURGERY CENTER

An outpatient surgery center is a freestanding center that provides planned, elective, outpatient surgical procedures, allowing a patient to recover and leave the center in most cases during the same day of surgery. The advantages of an outpatient surgery center are much lower cost and the convenience of a much quicker recovery. This is a real plus for most patients, especially for those without healthcare insurance. Most **health maintenance organizations** and Medicare pay for outpatient surgical center procedures, and in some states the state's Medicaid programs pay as well. In the surgicenter an added level of attention is paid to the patient, which aid in decreasing anxieties linked to having surgery. Physicians and surgeons are able to spend more time with each patient, providing quantity in addition to quality care.

Only surgeries that are not complicated or that do not require serious nursing care are performed in an outpatient surgicenter. Patients are made aware by their surgeon in advance that there are always risks and perhaps unexpected difficulties that may result in the patient having to be quickly hospitalized, although those occurrences are usually very rare.

The outpatient surgery center itself comprises several operating rooms complete with high-tech surgical equipment. There are separate areas for other stages of postoperative care.

Many surgicenters schedule their procedures on outpatients from 6:00 a.m. to 6:00 p.m., Monday through Friday, and many have Saturday hours. The recovery center may be open extended hours in the evening as needed.

TYPICAL PROCEDURES PERFORMED IN AN OUTPATIENT SURGERY CENTER

Different surgicenters perform different surgical procedures. Some of the more common ones include:

- Dental/oral surgery
- Breast biopsy
- **Laparoscopic surgery**
- Orthopedics
- Gynecology
- **Endoscopy, colonoscopy,** and sigmoidoscopy

OUTPATIENT SURGICAL CENTER STAFF

In addition to several highly skilled surgeons, the outpatient surgicenter team may be composed of the following:

- Anesthesiologist: This is a physician who is board certified in anesthesiology and is specifically trained in outpatient anesthesia. In some states, **certified registered nurse anesthetists (CRNAs)** are permitted to independently administer anesthesia, whereas in other states they must be supervised by an anesthesiologist who is physically available, though may be floating among several operating theaters. The anesthesiologist and/or the CRNA, along with the surgeon, meets with the patient in advance of surgery to discuss the surgery and address any questions or concerns the patient may have.

- Registered nurses: Nursing care in outpatient surgicenters is almost always provided by registered nurses in each operating theater. These registered and specially trained nurses provide preoperative and postoperative care to patients undergoing anesthesia during surgery. Other registered nurses assist surgeons by selecting and handling instruments, controlling bleeding, and assisting in the suturing of incisions.

- Surgical and radiology technologists: These registered technologists have experience in many surgical specialties and are often registered or otherwise certified, depending on the statutes of the state. Surgical technologists assist in setting up the operating room, ensuring that patients are transported to the operating theater, and sometimes assisting the surgeon in putting on gown and gloves. Radiology technologists take x-rays or administer nonradioactive materials into patients' bloodstreams for diagnostic purposes. Some specialize in diagnostic imaging technologies, such as computerized tomography and magnetic resonance imaging.

TYPICAL OUTPATIENT SURGICAL PROCEDURE: COLONOSCOPY

The patient usually arrives early in the morning on the day of the elective procedure. After completing necessary paperwork including insurance forms, routine Health Insurance Portability and Accountability Act confidentiality forms, and patient consent forms that give permission to allow the procedure, the patient is taken to a preparation area where the patient's valuables are secured or left with a family member. The patient is greeted, briefly measured (blood pressure, etc.), and then watched and monitored by several of the professional nursing staff. During this time there should be a brief preoperative interview by the CRNA or anesthesiologist. The patient is requested to change from his or her clothes to a convenient and comfortable gown, which has the necessary and appropriate openings to accommodate the surgery. The patient reclines on a gurney and an intravenous line may be started to allow for mild sedation, easing the patient into the otherwise strange environment. A short period may pass while the patient waits for the next available crew and operating theater to become vacant. He or she may then be transported on the same gurney to the operating room where heavier sedation is begun and the procedure undertaken.

At the conclusion of the procedure, the patient gradually awakens and may actually view a digital video of the procedure. For example, it would not be unusual, while still in the theater, to see a large pink cave or tunnel and realize that it is the patient's own bowel, the images captured on film or digitally during the colonoscopy procedure.

The patient is then transported, by gurney, to the recovery area and continuously monitored while further awakening. When the patient becomes able to sit, stand, and move, he or she changes from the patient gown back into his or her normal clothes. Usually, the physician drops by to provide an explanation of the findings, or in many instances the patient is told to plan a follow-up visit with his or her own primary physician. A report of the procedure is dictated by the physician who performed the procedure and then sent to the primary care physician, who may then discuss with the patient the next step in the patient's care. This could range from being told to repeat the procedure in 10 years, in the case of an uneventful colonoscopy, to being told that another procedure is in order.

CHAPTER SUMMARY

Outpatient surgery centers have proliferated in recent years, chiefly as a result of spiraling hospital costs. Countless procedures may be performed safely in these centers at great convenience to the patient and at great saving to the healthcare system. Many centers specialize in a few procedures (e.g., cataract surgery or colonoscopy), thus further decreasing costs and the time spent in the operating theater.

CHAPTER REVIEW

1. Why has the number of outpatient surgery centers recently grown rapidly?
2. May all surgical procedures be performed on an outpatient basis? Why or why not?
3. List a few common outpatient procedures.
4. Who are some of the team members you would expect to see in an outpatient surgery center?
5. Would nearly all outpatient surgical procedures be elective? Why or why not?

Discussion: A friend of yours who is 50 years old recently read a health article stating that colon cancer may be detected early through a simple colonoscopy procedure. The friend understands that you are a hospital administrator and inquires as to how many days they should expect to spend in your facility when the procedure is performed. What advice do you give your friend?

Chapter 16

Pain Management

Key Terms	
Patient-controlled analgesia pump	Transcutaneous electrical nerve
Physiatrist	stimulation (TENS) unit

Key Terms

Patient-controlled analgesia pump
Physiatrist

Transcutaneous electrical nerve
stimulation (TENS) unit

INTRODUCTION

Millions of people in America live with chronic pain. With baby boomers getting older, more and more people will live with chronic conditions causing pain. This can be a result of a traffic accident, a work-related injury, a genetic predisposition, or even reaching old age. In any event, the management of pain is something sought by the public, and treatment modalities come in many forms. In this chapter we discuss several different specialists and the forms of treatment, medicine, and options that patients may choose.

UNDERSTANDING YOUR PAIN

There are many symptoms and types of pain. It is important that the patient is able to explain his or her pain to the physician to get the proper diagnosis and correct treatment. The physician may clarify by asking the following questions: "Is the pain mild, sharp, dull, or severe?" "Is it stationary, does it move around, or does it only hurt at night?" "Is it a result of an injury like whiplash from a car accident, or is it chronic pain that you associate with a sports injury?" There are multiple questions for multiple categories of pain.

PSYCHOLOGISTS AND COPING METHODS

One important option is learning to live with pain. There may be little hope for a chronic pain sufferer simply because of the nature of the problem. An accident may have left him or her permanently injured for which no amount of surgery, physical therapy, or temporary relief from medications can offer a permanent remedy.

When this is true, relief may come in the form of group counseling. A psychologist will host a group of six to eight individuals who will share with the group their common problem in coping with their pain, relating how they came to have the problem, their strategies for pain management, and the progress they seem to be making. Support groups of this nature may be very effective for individuals to discover new methods to help with their own pain, with problems in sleeping, information on new products such as back pillows that may be used during work, or even placebos that work when conventional science says they should not.

A key ingredient in this form of therapy is, of course, the trained psychologist. This leader and counselor has experience with professional methodologies, has contacts with colleagues in other specialties to which he or she can refer, and has most likely seen numerous similar cases. Because a psychologist is not a medical doctor, he or she may likely obtain most of his or her patients from general practitioners who have examined the patient and know that surgery and other methods will be of limited use. Psychologists also have limited authority in writing prescriptions; this can vary depending on the statutes in the state in which the psychologist is practicing. The bottom line in psychology seems to be, "How can I learn to live with the pain that I know will likely not disappear?"

PHYSICAL MEDICINE, EXERCISE, AND PHYSIATRISTS

A **physiatrist** is a physician specializing in physical medicine and rehabilitation. This physician went to medical school, uses physical therapy, and treats the patient without surgery. Using this methodology, the physician works with the patient to build up and strengthen muscle groups that can help to alleviate problematic pain areas, which could be neck pain, back pain, carpal tunnel syndrome and other repetitive stress disorders, sciatica, pinched nerves, tendonitis, or even phantom pain.

An example of the use of a physiatrist is the following. After a fall, a patient has injured her shoulder and has limited range of motion of her arm. She cannot raise her left arm and hand high enough to brush her hair and has trouble getting dressed. This injury is painful throughout the day, coming and going as she undertakes activities of everyday living. Upon her referral to the physiatrist, she is examined, is perhaps referred to an imaging center for magnetic resonance imaging or CT scan to ensure this is a stretched ligament and not a rotator tear, and then a series of physical exercises are prescribed. She may be required to walk her fingers up and down a doorway at home to gradually strengthen her shoulder, which in turn eases the chronic pain. Additionally, she may be asked to work with weights to build up muscles to prevent future problems.

Physiatrists also play an important part in easing back pain. Many millions of people suffer from this pain because of ergonomic problems in their work area, degenerative discs due to aging, or perhaps from a traffic accident. By working to build and strengthen their back muscles, load bearing can increase and pain may decrease.

TRANSCUTANEOUS ELECTRICAL NERVE STIMULATION AND ELECTROTHERMAL THERAPY

Short-term pain may be managed and relieved by transcutaneous electrical nerve stimulation therapy; this is used many times for back pain. The **transcutaneous electrical nerve stimulation (TENS) unit** has electrodes that are attached to a small battery-operated mechanism that sends low-voltage electrical currents through the skin near the area of pain. Electricity passing through the electrodes sends a message to the brain to alleviate and provide relief from the pain.

DRUGS AND ANESTHESIOLOGISTS

To obtain immediate relief, patients may be referred to an anesthesiologist who is familiar with and trained in pain management. Anesthesiologists are the physicians usually seen in the operating theater who induce the patient into sleep so that surgery may be performed; however, the anesthesiologist may also have additional training and experience in pain relief.

A patient with chronic back pain may be referred to the anesthesiologist for an injection of drugs to numb the painful area in question. This injection, perhaps of cortisone, may not last for more than a few days and is usually not seen as a long-term solution. However, this treatment does provide needed immediate relief and may be sufficient for those seeking other types of therapy or for those who are recovering and for whom the pain is not likely to be permanent.

Along the same line as cortisone injections are pain pumps. A **patient-controlled analgesia pump** that contains a syringe of doctor-prescribed pain medication is connected directly to a patient's intravenous line. Some pumps deliver a constant flow of pain medication, and some are controlled by requiring the patient to press a button. Patient-controlled analgesia pumps contain a safety mechanism to prevent the patient from administering an unsafe level of pain medication.

Several years ago it was thought that a miracle drug had arrived in the form of cyclooxygenase-2 inhibitors. Initially, it was believed that these medications were the answer to chronic pain from arthritis, osteoarthritis, and other painful conditions. They were found to be more potent than other anti-inflammatory drugs such as naproxen and ibuprofen. Their use was short-lived, however, when it was discovered they were linked to heart, stroke, and ulcer risks, and all but one of the more popular medications were removed from use.

SURGERY AND SURGEONS

Another solution that pain sufferers may use is that of surgery. Often, a painful problem may require surgical repair, for example, in a situation similar to the one previously cited of the patient with the injured shoulder. In the new case, the patient is seen, through the use of an MRI, to have a torn rotator cuff instead of merely stretched ligaments. With this painful condition, physical exercise may exacerbate the injury instead of relieving the pain.

In this case the patient is referred to a surgeon who, after careful examination and discussion with the radiologist who read the magnetic resonance images, consults with the patient and plans the surgery. The torn rotator cuff is reattached, the patient undertakes rehabilitation exercises, and the shoulder is restored close to its original function, minus the chronic pain.

ALTERNATIVE MEDICINE AND PAIN MANAGEMENT

Intended to work in conjunction with conventional medicine, alternative or complementary medicine promotes choices such as:

- Acupuncture
- Meditation
- Deep breathing and stress management
- Mind–body connection through positive thinking
- Massage and other approaches to pain relief

PAIN MANAGEMENT AT THE END OF LIFE

Many patients in advanced stages of cancer or those with acquired immunodeficiency syndrome (AIDS) find themselves with severe pain. The patient knows the extent of his or her pain and is assisted through a series of interviewing techniques designed to accurately describe their pain:

- Describe the pain and show me where it hurts.
- How severe is the pain and does it keep you awake?

- On a scale of 1 to 10, with 10 being unbearable and the worse you have ever encountered and 1 being barely noticeable, how would you rank your pain in each of the areas that you described?

A plan is then designed by the physician to assist the patient to cope with his or her pain. A plan that is not effective in controlling the patient's pain must be reassessed to make the patient as comfortable as possible.

Patients with serious illness often are afraid of having uncontrolled or inadequately controlled pain. Past practices feared addiction to narcotic painkillers and frequently caused a patient to suffer needlessly. Though some narcotic painkillers cause addiction, if used in a controlled setting, the benefits far outweigh the risks for abuse.

CHAPTER SUMMARY

Many people suffer acute and chronic pain. There are a host of physicians and non-physicians, treatments, exercises, drugs, and even surgeries to correct these problems. This chapter has discussed psychology and psychologists, physiatrist and physical medicine, anesthesiologists and drugs, and surgery and surgeons. Patients usually want to start with a conservative approach to their problem and only move to invasive procedures when relief is not found. Even though one has chronic pain, there is no reason to suffer if provided with proper pain management tools.

CHAPTER REVIEW

1. What is a physiatrist and how would you expect him or her to help a patient complaining of pain?
2. How would you expect an anesthesiologist to help a patient complaining of pain?
3. How could group therapy be helpful for those patients with chronic pain?
4. Should surgery be the last resort in the management of pain? Why or why not?
5. Are there other methods of pain management that you are familiar with? Why should the onset of pain be something for which you should immediately seek the advice of your physician?

Discussion: Your father has recently been involved in a traffic accident and is now complaining of pain in both his neck and his right leg. He seeks your advice regarding what type of physician he should see. What advice do you give him?

Chapter 17

Physical and Rehabilitation Medicine

Key Terms

Occupational therapy

Physical therapy

Recreational therapy

Rehabilitation medicine

Sports medicine

Work hardening

INTRODUCTION

Rehabilitation medicine is that field of medicine that assists patients in achieving the state of well-being that existed before an accident, injury, heart attack, stroke, cancer, or other malady that left the patient in an altered state of physical well-being. This area of medicine may take many forms; physical therapy, occupational therapy, sports medicine, recreational therapy, cardiac rehabilitation, and work hardening are some of these areas.

PHYSICAL THERAPY

Many weekend athletes find themselves barely able to walk, much less go to work when Monday morning rolls around. After a visit to the family physician, an orthopedic surgeon, or sometimes a chiropractor, the patient is given a referral to a **physical therapy** practice for some quick (or depending on the injury, not so quick) physical rehabilitation.

Physical therapists are those professionals who have completed graduate school in physical therapy and then taken a state examination to become licensed in the field of physical therapy. These therapists, usually working from a physician referral, examine and interview the patient. The therapist may determine that hot packs and massage are a good beginning to relieve pain and relax the patient, preparing him or her for exercises that are to follow. Physical therapists are also very important in the treatment of severe burn patients, working to care for the burn while the patient is in a water bath.

After determining the correct exercise and, usually, physical exercise machines to use, the physical therapist demonstrates for the patient how the exercise or machine is to be used. The patient then undertakes a series of exercises while the physical therapist encourages and works with the patient to assist in overcoming the injury.

Common modalities of physical therapy can include "gait training" to assist those who are learning to walk again, hydrotherapy using warm to hot water and whirlpool motion, and even common mat exercises on the floor, whatever it takes to assist the patient, ease the pain, enhance the muscular skeletal system, and get the person past the physical injury that can be debilitating and limiting of life's activities.

OCCUPATIONAL THERAPY

Occupational therapy is that field of allied health that assists people in improving their ability to perform tasks in their daily work and living environment. These patients may be physically, mentally, developmentally, or emotionally challenged; the occupational therapist helps the patient to improve basic motor functions and reasoning abilities and to also compensate for what is sometimes the permanent loss of these abilities.

Occupational therapy treatment can include performing activities of everyday living such as cooking, dressing, or even eating. Physical exercises may increase strength and dexterity to improve eye–hand coordination. Occupational therapists can work with spinal cord injuries and with adaptive equipment to include orthopedic devices, wheelchairs, or aids for eating and dressing. Occupational therapists may spend time studying the living situation to assist in identifying hazards and environmental factors that could contribute to falls. They can also teach shopping, budgeting, homemaking, and the use of public transportation to those who may be mentally challenged.

SPORTS MEDICINE

Sports medicine has become popular during the last two decades as a way to cater to teenagers and adults who vigorously pursue softball, basketball, hockey, and other sports that may involve injury-producing activities. Whereas college teams have professional team trainers, weekend athletes have the family physician, who often refers the injured weekend athlete to someone specifically trained in the clinical and scientific aspects of exercise and sports. This area of medicine has seen a huge increase as aging baby boomers seek care to continue their physical goals and sports aspirations.

Sports medicine may involve research into the physiological, behavioral, biomechanical, or even biochemical facets of exercise. The goal is to prevent or diagnose and treat physical injuries or to improve performance when possible.

RECREATIONAL THERAPY

Recreational therapists use leisure activities to maintain and improve their patient's general well-being and health. These activities can include arts and crafts, sports, games, dance, music, or even animals. **Recreational therapy** techniques may assist in reducing stress, depression, and anxiety and help to build confidence, socialization skills, and assist in reducing or eliminating effects of illness or disability.

CARDIAC REHABILITATION

Cardiac rehabilitation is a medically supervised intervention program with the targeted purpose of limiting physical damage from heart disease. Primarily using exercise and education, cardiac rehabilitation is generally considered by experts to be a mandatory part of the discharge plan of every heart disease patient. Benefits of cardiac rehabilitation can include:

1. Increased tolerance to exercise
2. Decreased angina pain, shortness of breath, and fatigue
3. Improved cholesterol levels
4. Decreased desire to continue smoking
5. Reduction of stress and enhanced psychosocial well-being
6. Enhanced longevity

Cardiac rehabilitation usually consists of 4 to 12 weeks of progressive aerobic conditioning and may also include resistance training. Education is a mandatory part that usually contains dietetic counseling, if necessary a smoking cessation program, and lifestyle changes to encourage regular exercise.

WORK HARDENING

A special function of physical medicine is **work hardening**, a relatively new allied health field designed to get injured workers ready to return to the workplace. A therapist in work hardening carefully interviews and listens to the patient describe his or her work setting and then formulates appropriate tasks and exercises to ready the patient for returning to work. As an example, if the injured patient has a hand injury and was a mechanic who often uses a screwdriver, he or she may find themselves standing before a large wooden board with numerous protruding wood screws. The patient is instructed to engage in the task of screwing each wood screw into the board to build strength in the injured hand, in turn becoming ready to return to his or her job.

CHAPTER SUMMARY

Rehabilitative medicine can take many forms. Physical therapy may assist patients in strengthening muscles so that the patient gets back to his or her everyday life as it existed before the injury. Occupational therapy may assist patients with skills for everyday living such as cooking, skills needed to make correct change, or using public transportation. Recreational therapy may assist patients by teaching arts, crafts, music, or dance. Cardiac rehabilitation is for patients who have had a myocardial infarction and need to enhance their damaged heart muscle; this can include a regimen of exercise, smoking cessation, and lifestyle change. Work hardening is an important area of rehabilitative medicine designed to build the physical skills needed for a patient to return to his or her work setting as it was before the injury.

CHAPTER REVIEW

1. Describe the rehabilitation program that might be presented to patients after they have had a heart attack.
2. Describe the rehabilitation program that might be presented to ready a patient to return to work if the worker was a carpenter before the injury.
3. If a patient was a weekend scuba diver and found he or she was having leg cramps after using his or her fins, who could offer the best exercise program?
4. Describe a rehabilitative program for long-term care patients that might aid in lifting their depression.
5. Describe the types of patients that a physical therapist might treat.

Discussion: A friend of yours has been involved in a motor vehicle accident and is complaining of severe neck pain. After examination, to whom is her physician likely to refer her for follow-up care? What course of treatment is likely to follow?

Chapter 18

Psychology, Psychiatry, and Alternative Forms of Psychotherapy

<table>
<tr><td colspan="2" align="center">Key Terms</td></tr>
<tr><td>Art therapy</td><td>Psychologists</td></tr>
<tr><td>Behavior therapy</td><td>Psychotherapy</td></tr>
<tr><td>Psychiatrist</td><td></td></tr>
</table>

INTRODUCTION

The brain is an organ, as is the heart, pancreas, and lungs. It may act within what has been deemed to be normal limits, or it may act within what has been judged to be abnormal. Many believe that about 20% of the U.S. population, or 1 in 5, need help, assistance, or counseling in some manner for mental problems. Assistance may be simple, as in a need to speak with one's religious leader, school counselor, or support group, or it may be more serious and require therapy and medication. This chapter explores different forms of treatment that are available in an outpatient setting.

PSYCHOLOGY

Psychology is both an academic and an applied field that studies the mind and behavior. Research in this field attempts to understand emotions, behavior, and thought. Applied psychology may engage in mental health treatment, performance improvement, or other areas impacting on daily life and health.

Psychologists achieve an undergraduate education and then attend graduate school, pursuing a PhD or PsyD in counseling or clinical psychology. These doctoral programs may take 5 to 7 years to complete. In some states, an additional internship of 1 or 2 years is needed, whereas in other states perhaps a couple of years of supervised practice is needed before a license is awarded.

Traditionally, psychologists may not prescribe medications, but recently there has been a move in some states to modify this, usually if the psychologist first consults with a psychiatrist. Psychologists typically administer psychological tests, conduct psychotherapy, and conduct research.

PSYCHIATRY

A **psychiatrist** is someone who has 4 years of college, 4 years of medical school and becomes an MD or DO, and then completes another 4 years of residency training in the diagnosis, treatment, and prevention of mental illness. On top of this, some choose to specialize and receive even more training in areas such as addictions, child, adolescent, or geriatric psychiatry. A psychiatrist is a licensed physician, practices medicine, and may prescribe medications or the use of hospitalization for extensive problems.

PSYCHOTHERAPY

Psychotherapy is a general word for treating emotional disorders by talking with a mental health professional. It can be an array of services used to alleviate symptoms of anger or hopelessness to regain enjoyment, balance, and control of one's life. Forms that psychotherapy may take are as follows:

- Psychoanalysis: This modality involves talking with a psychoanalyst for several sessions a week perhaps for a year or several years. In this treatment, patients typically may be guided to explore their conscious or unconscious thoughts in an attempt to understand, treat, and improve their life.
- **Art therapy** or creative art therapy: Patients who find art or creative therapy helpful may have problems expressing their feelings or thoughts. Forms of this therapy include drawing, painting, music, and dance. Art therapy is thought to increase self-awareness, cope with traumatic experiences, and thus foster positive changes.
- **Behavior therapy:** Some individuals experience anxiety, fear, or discomfort, and behavior therapy seeks to overcome these through a system of rewards or through the reinforcement of positive behavior. Desensitization is also another technique used to treat anxiety or fear; with this technique the person is often introduced to a series of confrontations to help overcome his or her fears.

CHAPTER SUMMARY

Problems of the mind are no different from problems with other organs or diseases of other organs; they may be successfully treated through counseling, therapy, or the use of medication. Psychologists are trained in recognizing mental disorders and then in working with the patient or client to overcome these problems and to reach a more normal state of being. Psychiatrists are, in addition, medical doctors trained in recognizing mental disorders and then treating the patient through prescribing medications and using counseling techniques to assist the patient to reach a more normal state of mental well-being.

CHAPTER REVIEW

1. You notice that a friend of yours is excessively drinking and last night was stopped on the way home by the police, though only given a warning to go straight home. Whom would you suggest your friend see for help?
2. You have a friend who seems to have excessive test anxiety, even though he studies much more than you. This may be a problem in that he paces, doesn't sleep, and even tries to read his text while driving. Who would you suggest he visit for help?
3. Your friend's mother seems to have a phobia for spiders. She shakes her shoes before putting them on, asks others to open kitchen drawers and examine them, and now refuses to vacuum. What should she probably do regarding her problem?
4. What is the difference between a psychologist and a psychiatrist?
5. Your grandfather seems to be forgetful, but recently much more so. You have considered that this may simply a problem of aging, but you now realize that his father had Alzheimer's disease. Whom do you suggest he see?

Discussion: A friend of yours confides in you that he feels his mail is being read by other people, someone is usually following him, and his telephone conversations are usually listened to by others. To whom would you likely refer him for assistance?

Chapter 19

Protecting the Public's Health—Efforts at Every Level

Key Terms

Centers for Disease Control and
   Prevention (CDC)
Environmental Protection Agency (EPA)
Food and Drug Administration (FDA)
Occupational Safety and Health
   Administration (OSHA)

Public health
Severe acute respiratory
   syndrome (SARS)

INTRODUCTION

Public health is an all-encompassing term that serves a tremendous purpose in American health care. Besides the macro federal effort of agencies such as **Centers for Disease Control and Prevention (CDC)**, the **Food and Drug Administration (FDA)**, the **Environmental Protection Agency (EPA)**, and the **Occupational Safety and Health Administration (OSHA)**, all states and cities have ongoing smaller agencies to provide a myriad of sanitation services and inspections. On an even more micro level, cities provide prenatal care, dental care, and a host of services to serve and safeguard the health of each citizen.

PUBLIC HEALTH, OCCUPATIONAL HEALTH, AND ENVIRONMENTAL HEALTH

It may seem odd to include this area of health care in a book that usually discusses where consumers may turn for particular services such as travel medicine, pain management, or long-term care. However, public health is such a cornerstone of health care that we often overlook it and have come to take it for granted.

As America approached the 21st century, there began to be a host of magazine and news articles that asked the public to speculate, "In your opinion, what was the greatest invention or event of the last 100 years? Was it the computer, could it be landing on the moon, perhaps the civil rights movement?" Just as many people answered with a host of favorite ideas, many missed the most obvious of all answers: advances in public health. The below 10 events have added 30+ years to the average life span (MMWR, 1999):

1. Vaccinations
2. Advances in motor vehicle safety
3. Safer workplaces
4. Control of infectious diseases
5. Decline in heart disease and strokes through better health education
6. Safer and healthier foods
7. Healthier mothers and babies
8. Advances in family planning
9. Fluoridation of drinking water
10. Recognition of tobacco as a health hazard

In addition, there are public health efforts today at the federal, state, and city level that focus on protecting clean air; safeguarding drinking water; eliminating hazardous waste; inspecting restaurants, food establishments, and grocery stores; safeguarding children from dangerous toys; inspecting meat, vegetables, and dairy products at the site of production; safeguarding pharmaceutical products; and safeguarding the workplace.

Another macro impact of public health is that it is the first line of defense from sudden acute disease as the world undergoes globalization. For example, a similar epidemic to the bird flu or the **severe acute respiratory syndrome (SARS)** epidemic could spread quickly from China or Thailand to Los Angeles or New York through air travel. Only the CDC or other federal programs could have the massive resources to inoculate vulnerable populations quickly. Hospitals may not be the focal point of health care; quarantine may be a more logical protection and logical choice against mass casualties.

PUBLIC HEALTH CLINICS

Because the focus of this book is "outside the hospital," we turn our examination to a more micro level. Where can less affluent members of the public seek care? What is an economically challenged member of society to do when she finds herself pregnant, addicted to drugs, or human immunodeficiency virus (HIV) positive (or all three)?

Many cities have public health clinics to provide assistance. Though often the waiting time for an appointment may be long, prenatal care may be available for those that seek care. This use of prenatal care can reduce the number of premature infants who would otherwise be of greater expense to society and who could also experience lifelong health problems.

In addition to prenatal care, many cities are hosting drug treatment centers. By acknowledging that individuals need care, these centers can work to diminish addiction and, in turn, can work to diminish HIV that may be spread through shared needles. Indeed, sexually transmitted diseases gained new attention when they became life threatening in the 1980s in the form of HIV and then acquired immunodeficiency syndrome. No longer were they treatable by a shot of penicillin. Public health clinics gained new importance.

Public dental clinics also provide an outlet for the economically disadvantaged. Dental hygiene can help to ensure overall good health.

CHAPTER SUMMARY

A measure of society is how well it cares for its most vulnerable population. Public health efforts, whether in a macro format such as air pollution or disease control or in a micro format of assisting one mother at a time, are important to society's entire well-being.

CHAPTER REVIEW

1. What agencies at the federal level are designed to ensure good overall health and well-being?
2. What are some state and local agencies that protect the individual health of citizens?
3. Where could an economically challenged, pregnant teen expect to find prenatal care?
4. Why are sexually transmitted disease clinics more important today than in the past?
5. What is the federal OSHA designed to protect?

Discussion: A family that you know has recently had a bout of bad luck and found themselves without work. Advise them on their options for receiving dental and prenatal care.

REFERENCE

(1999). *Morbidity and Mortality Weekly Review, 48,* 241–243.

Chapter 20

Sleep Disorders

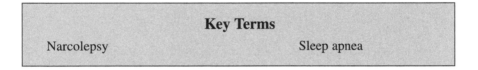

Key Terms

Narcolepsy   Sleep apnea

INTRODUCTION

Nearly everyone has problems sleeping at some time in their life. A true sleep disorder is when this condition persists and seemingly will not go away. Many people seek the help of their physician who may often refer them to a physician specializing in diagnosing and treating sleep disorders. This physician may advise them to keep a sleep journal for a couple of weeks; if there seems to be a problem, the patient may be referred to a specialist or to a sleep disorder center.

COMMON SLEEP DISORDERS

Insomnia is a disorder in which patients have trouble maintaining sleep or in going to sleep. They may wake during the night and then have trouble returning to sleep. They may wake too early every morning or even feel unrefreshed after sleeping. This may lead to sleepiness during the day while working or otherwise interfere with daytime activities.

There are several different types of insomnia. Transient insomnia may be a response to temporary stress, anxiety before an examination, excitement the night before a vacation, or an unfamiliar environment such as an extra hard motel bed while traveling. The bout of insomnia subsides after the events or environment returns to normal. Short-term insomnia occurs during longer periods, perhaps a few weeks, and can go away when the stressor or event subsides. Chronic insomnia can be a pattern of sleeplessness lasting for a longer period. Sufferers may

101

have problems relating to other people and/or may be too tired to perform well on the job. All these conditions may be attributable to medications, a medical condition, or a very stressful environment.

Obstructive **sleep apnea** is usually deemed a very serious sleep disorder. In the most common form, the upper airway becomes blocked or obstructed during sleep (most often when the soft tissue in the rear of the throat constricts or collapses during sleep), causing a cessation of breathing for as much as 90 seconds. People may experience this many times each night while sleeping. During each episode, the person wakes or nearly wakes and then goes back to sleep. Identifying signs may be snoring, waking up frequently, obesity, high blood pressure, and headaches in the morning; of course, this condition is accompanied with daytime fatigue. In the less common form, central sleep apnea, the brain fails to cause the muscles to breathe; this is believed to be due to respiratory control center instability. It is labeled central apnea because of the connection to the central nervous system.

Narcolepsy is a disorder that affects the control of wakefulness and sleep. Sufferers experience excessive sleepiness in the daytime and often uncontrollable episodes of sleeping during the day, often in meetings, at their job, or even during meals. It may go undiagnosed and therefore not treated. Though rare, symptoms can appear acutely (suddenly) or develop slowly over a lengthy duration. Recognized sufferers are cautioned not to operate a motor vehicle.

Restless leg syndrome is the rhythmic jerking of feet and/or legs, causing patients to move their legs. Patients may have tingling, cramping, or irritation that causes them to want to walk around to relieve the symptoms; of course, this is very disruptive to sleep patterns.

DIAGNOSING AND TREATING SLEEP DISORDERS

After keeping a sleep diary and having it reviewed by a general practitioner, often a patient is referred to a sleep disorder center. Sleep centers may be under the direction of a pulmonology specialist because of the large number of breathing problems that are related to sleep disorders.

If a sleep study is suggested, the patient may arrive in the evening with his or her sleepwear, usually finding the sleep study room to be decorated and furnished much like a regular bedroom. A technician may place leads on the patient to perform a polysomnogram (PSG) study, which is a multiple-component test that measures and records various physical activities while the patient sleeps. The readings are then analyzed by a qualified practitioner to determine whether a sleep disorder exists and, if one does, the nature of the disorder. For example, breathing patterns that simply cease several times during sleep may indicate sleep apnea. The patient may be given a prescription to purchase a machine to assist with breathing during the night and then be advised to lose weight.

CHAPTER SUMMARY

Sleep disorders may be temporary due to anxiety or may be chronic and the symptom of a more serious illness. These disorders can be examined through carefully monitored sleep studies. The patient may be prescribed medication, given advice on ways to enhance sleep, or even prescribed equipment to assist with breathing.

CHAPTER REVIEW

1. What are some common causes of the temporary inability to sleep well?
2. What are causes of sleep apnea?
3. What is restless leg syndrome?
4. What is narcolepsy and how can it be dangerous?
5. Why can chronic insomnia be a serious illness?

Discussion: Your friend has recently had trouble sleeping and now finds himself dozing during class. Should you suggest anything to assist him in his endeavors to acquire sleep?

Chapter 21

Travel Medicine

INTRODUCTION

Many millions of Americans travel abroad each year, either on business or on holiday. It is usual for them to spend about 2 weeks, but many find themselves ill for a few days during their travels.

To meet the needs of these citizens who journey forth, "travel medicine" started in the mid-1980s. These specialty clinics counsel people on the potential of illnesses in particular areas, offer travel advice, and sell inoculations that may be appropriate to the destination of the traveler.

TRAVEL INTELLIGENCE AND ADVICE

The travel medicine clinic may be a wonderful source of information for precautions to take when traveling, especially to developing countries where even water from the faucet is not safe to drink. Brushing one's teeth without using bottled water may lead to severe illness for several days, causing travel plans to be changed or, in more severe cases, a brief period of hospitalization in a foreign land where little English may be spoken.

Travel advice is especially needed for the pregnant traveler, those with special healthcare needs, children, or the older traveler. Many of the professionals who are attracted to employment in travel medicine clinics are often frequent travelers themselves. If a travel medicine clinic is not available to the person about to journey, both the **World Health Organization** and the Centers for Disease Control and Prevention have comprehensive websites that can be helpful (www.who.int and www.cdc.gov/travel). Both sites list topics such as vaccinations, diseases, and safe food/water and show maps of travel destinations that are updated with health warnings. Also, local or county health departments often have travel medicine clinics that provide pre-travel information.

Many vacationers travel specifically to dive or to climb in high altitudes. Special knowledge and precautions are necessary to prevent air-related bends (flying in small unpressurized airplanes while island hopping between dives) or to determine the time necessary to acclimate to prevent high-altitude sickness in certain mountain ranges. The travel medicine clinic can be a gold mine of intelligence for the traveler to assess not only health risks at the destination, but also risky behavior that should be avoided.

INOCULATIONS AND VACCINES

In many parts of the world, yellow fever, meningitis, cholera, and other diseases rare in the United States are all too common. Vaccines and inoculations are usually available on site to be administered from the travel medicine clinic. The traveler is advised to seek these early because several vaccines require two to three shots to complete a series. Even a single shot may take at least 10 days to produce the correct immunity. Questionnaires should be completed ahead of the scheduled appointment to provide necessary information and to ensure that relevant issues in the traveler's medical history are not overlooked. The medical provider should find out as much about the trip as possible to tailor the travel health advice to the individual. The traveler is then adequately prepared and has the necessary information of how to protect his or her health.

An official immunization record should be given to the traveler to carry with his or her passport. Although not required by all countries, proof of having the necessary shots can be helpful when crossing certain borders.

RECOMMENDED EQUIPMENT, SUPPLIES, AND PRODUCTS

Travel medicine clinics can also recommend the latest in lightweight clothing and correct boots or shoes, mosquito repellents (extremely helpful in avoiding malaria, one of the world's leading causes of deaths), portable water purifiers, and antidiarrheal kits. The clinic can advise on packing the correct items to complete a travel medicine kit. Also available are specially designed travel health plans, security briefings, travel health insurance, and even services for groups. These services can also provide information on contacting English-speaking physicians and locating competent medical facilities in the area that is targeted for travel.

POST-TRAVEL MEDICAL CARE

Most travel medicine clinics offer post-travel medical care in addition to pre-travel care. For example, a traveler may return from the Far East displaying flu-like symptoms and a high fever. The first step for the travel medicine clinician is to determine the patient's recent travel history. That would provide a major clue to rule out malaria, which could require emergency care.

RESPONSIBLE TRAVEL

The search for engaging customs, exciting safaris, exotic foods, or fascinating destinations can be any traveler's dream; however, it should be tempered with planning, preparation, the correct information (weather, political instability, annoying insects and vermin, health care, etc.), and necessary vaccinations to make the journey enjoyable, healthy, and safe. The motivation for future travel is guided by a healthy trip and a positive experience.

CHAPTER SUMMARY

As more and more venture to foreign countries, travel medicine has become a near subspecialty clinic practice. Specializing in unique information of indigenous diseases and pests and having the correct knowledge and on-hand supply of the right vaccines, the travel medicine clinic may be the difference between an enjoyable trip and one spent in a foreign hospital bed.

CHAPTER REVIEW

1. List at least five health services that a travel medicine clinic can offer that a primary physician may not.
2. When would you likely want the services of a travel medicine clinic after traveling?
3. Why is it necessary to consult a travel medicine clinic well in advance of traveling?
4. Is water always safe from a kitchen or bathroom tap, even for brushing your teeth?
5. Besides advice on diseases and pests, what else are you likely to learn from the personnel at a travel medicine clinic?

Discussion: A friend of yours has accepted employment in Shanghai, China, a very modern city of approximately 15 million people. Should she get advice from a travel medicine clinic? Why?

Chapter 22

Weight Loss

<table>
<tr><td colspan="2" align="center">**Key Terms**</td></tr>
<tr><td>Body mass index (BMI)
Gastric banding</td><td>Obesity</td></tr>
</table>

INTRODUCTION

The United States, and for that matter the developed world, is increasingly becoming more obese. As most are aware, the Western diet of fast food, high fat, and enormous portions and sedentary lifestyles (Internet, television, video games, etc.) have added pounds and problems with cardiovascular diseases such as high blood pressure, diabetes, sleep apnea, and other health- and food-related issues.

One solution to this epidemic might lie in government policy, such as mandatory physical education for children. In October 2007, Texas became the first state in many years to enact such a bill, ensuring that each child receives one-half hour of physical training each day. Other solutions, of course, lie within, but lack of education, lack of time to prepare nutritious meals, and the heavy influence of advertising make this "self-inflicted disease" (a disease that we can directly control) hard to control.

The **body mass index (BMI)** can be easy to use and a helpful indicator to check one's general health and as a way to monitor progress regarding weight loss. This simple-to-use table or wheel can be found in many bookstores, online, and certainly in physician offices. By measuring height and weight and then using them in conjunction with the BMI chart, the BMI is indicated. Those within the range of 21 to 24 are considered normal and those with 40 or greater, morbidly obese (usually considered to be 100 pounds or more over the ideal weight).

TREATMENT OPTIONS

There are many treatment options available, such as exercise programs, dietary supplements, and surgery. Some methods are more useful than others.

After cookbooks, diet books and exercise videos are probably the most popular selling materials in book stores. Overweight individuals viewing commercials see the marketing agency's perfectly sculptured bodies and want to emulate them. Instead of engaging in the best known exercise (gripping the dinner table and pushing backward instead of continuing to eat), the person fibs to him- or herself ("I'll stop tomorrow") and then spends $19.95 on the latest program, only to sell it at the neighborhood garage sale 2 months later, still in the original wrapper.

Home exercise equipment can be a convenient way to exercise, although many times the equipment isn't used, and the exercise program fails.

Meal substitute drinks are another option; they are low-calorie drinks that serve as meal replacements. These "Drink and Lose Now!" products promise to take inches and pounds off nutritionally, sometimes even overnight. Self-promises and New Year's resolutions extend to leaving one's brown paper bag lunch at home and in the alternative, ingesting the cream or goo in the can.

After trying to fight and losing the battle of the bulge, many go to their neighbor pharmacist or their physician to secure medications (i.e., diet pills) to assist in weight loss. These tablets, pills, or capsules are likely to have a modest effect, helping with 5 to 10 pounds of loss, but there are side effects that may be troublesome. Users expect magic bullet pills that melt fat; however, unless the person changes the dual harmful habits of continual eating and living a sedentary lifestyle, often when he or she stops taking the medications the pounds come back.

There are a host of commercial programs that charge a membership fee and then offer education and counseling, a support group, and "delicious" low-calorie meals aimed at weight loss. Like other methods, these programs work if peole are intent on changing their intake and consumption habits (overeating and incorrect eating) and breaking their sedentary routine.

As a strategy to lose weight, many people enroll in a fitness center or join a gymnasium. These centers can provide a host of activities at all hours of a day. For example, one might expect to find a swimming pool, whirlpool and sauna, stationary exercise equipment (treadmills and bicycles with televisions to watch the news while exercising), aerobic equipment, free weights, cooking, tai chi and martial arts classes, a health food and juice bar, and even an athletic shoe and clothing store. Many of these centers also offer the services of a personal trainer.

Medical weight loss centers are medical practice centers that employ physicians to professionally address the many issues of weight loss. Patients may seek help for simple cosmetic reasons or because their poor health habits lead to high blood pressure, diabetes, or other weight-related diseases. Patients may be counseled by a registered dietitian on correct eating habits, nutrition, and low-calorie diet programs. They are counseled on particular nuances of their illness by a physician's assistant or nurse practitioner and will most assuredly be subjected to a battery of diagnostic laboratory tests. Patients can expect to be presented with information on fitness, behavioral modification, and the dangers of **obesity** and then may qualify for a medication from the physician in charge to assist with their weight loss. They may expect a referral to a support group or exercise program in a nearby fitness center.

Weight loss surgery (also called bypass surgery, **gastric banding**, or obesity surgery) requires a hospital inpatient stay and thus is outside the range of this text, but a few paragraphs are devoted to this topic to round out the discussion regarding weight loss. Weight loss surgery is an alteration to the digestive system to restrict food intake and ensure smaller quantities of food are ingested and thus fewer calories processed.

Gastric bypass surgery is often done by the technique of laparoscopic surgery, making use of several small incisions. A viewing device may be introduced through one small opening, a light source through another, and instruments through another. The surgeon watches his or her own procedure on a video screen. Advantages of laparoscopic surgery may be a shorter recovery time, a reduced hospital stay, less scarring, and reduced chances of infections. Of course, disadvantages are the same as those with any surgery as well as the inconvenience of more frequent bowel movements.

During the surgery a small egg-size pouch is created from the upper stomach and the remaining portion of the stomach is bypassed. The patient will then feel very full after consuming only a small quantity of food, thus consuming less food and fewer calories. As mentioned earlier, this procedure is usually for the morbidly obese to address very serious health-related risks.

CHAPTER SUMMARY

Obesity is a major health issue, ranking with the use of tobacco products. There are a host of remedies available, ranging from exercise programs and dietary supplements to more severe methods such as gastric banding. This epidemic, driven by poor eating habits and sedentary lifestyles, unless soon changed, will have a major health effect on the nation, including increased cardiovascular disease and diabetes.

CHAPTER REVIEW

1. What are the self-inflicted causes of obesity?
2. What are two simple measures to combat being overweight?

3. What are additional measures that someone who is overweight might use to lose weight?
4. What are the dangers of gastric banding?
5. What is a BMI and what BMI is considered normal?

Discussion: You have a friend that is moderately overweight. What treatment options are available to her?

Chapter 23

Wellness Centers

INTRODUCTION

Health and **wellness** centers or clinics are often sponsored by physicians and hospitals as a way to enhance awareness of good health and to prevent illness and self-inflicted diseases such as tobacco-related cancers or alcohol-related psoriasis of the liver. These clinics may also improve the emotional and mental health of many clinic members.

WELLNESS CENTER OPTIONS

A wellness center is just that, a center that encourages and promotes all aspects of well-being to include physical, mental, and emotional good health. Many different services may be offered:

- Stationary bicycles and treadmills with headphones, arranged in front of large or individual television monitors
- Cardiac rehabilitation equipment to serve the recovering heart attack patient
- Machines designed to stress and improve nearly every individual muscle in the body
- Free weights to improve muscle tone
- Cooking classes to teach better, more healthy eating

- Lifestyle seminars to include weight loss and to encourage exercise
- Tai chi, karate, judo, aerobics, dance, physical fitness programs, and court sports
- Smoking cessation classes
- Awareness of complementary healthcare procedures such as acupuncture and chiropractic care
- Aquatic exercise, swimming, water ballet, and other water sports such as scuba diving lessons
- Steam room, whirlpool, and sauna
- Spa and body care treatments to include hair, nails, skin care, and massage therapy

Personal trainers may often offer new members an assessment of their well-being (i.e., how many pounds they may be overweight or helping to identify and target for change questionable lifestyle choices). A history and physical can uncover problems to watch, for example, thirst and frequent urination if there is a history of diabetes in the family. An exercise program can be tailored to the person and personal goals. By feeling part of an encouraging health group, his or her emotional and mental health may immediately begin improving.

CHAPTER SUMMARY

A wellness center can promote longevity, better health, and enjoyment of life. Cooking classes, exercise programs, and general health education can help to promote better health and lead away from poor eating and a sedentary lifestyle.

CHAPTER REVIEW

1. What are some programs that enhance health that you might expect to find at a wellness center?
2. What is some equipment that you might expect to find?
3. Why should people get into the habit of exercising and eating healthy?
4. List at least five water-related programs that you would expect to find in a wellness center.
5. What are some reasons not to go to a wellness center?

Discussion: You have been told by your physician that you have an above normal risk of diabetes due to being overweight and the fact that both of your parents had the disease. How can a wellness center help you?

Part IV
Chronic Care

Chapter 24

Dialysis

Key Terms

Hemodialysis   Peritoneal dialysis

INTRODUCTION

Kidney failure usually occurs from high blood pressure or from diabetes. It often occurs after about 10 years of kidney damage. The kidneys can no longer adequately filter waste from the blood. Dialysis is a method to filter wastes from the blood and body, mechanically using filters (**hemodialysis**) or by using a membrane inside the body (**peritoneal dialysis**).

People in good health have normal functioning kidneys that accomplish this. Blood circulates, passes through the kidney, and wastes are filtered. Others with more compromised kidneys, such as long-term diabetics or people with end-stage renal diseases, must seek a kidney transplant or dialysis care; otherwise, they may die.

Acute renal failure can be caused by dehydration, blood loss, or certain medications. The underlying cause is corrected, and the patient is given dialysis until the kidney's proper functions are restored.

Chronic kidney disease may occur during the course of many years, growing slowly worse over time. There are usually no symptoms until severe chronic kidney disease begins to cause fluid buildup and electrolyte imbalances, leading to kidney failure and the need for dialysis or a kidney transplant.

KIDNEY TRANSPLANTS

Organ transplantation is beyond the scope of this book, because it occurs "inside the hospital." However, the issues surrounding transplantation are briefly discussed to build awareness of this important issue.

Kidney transplants from living donors are by far the most preferable form of treating those with nonviable kidneys. Second to this are transplanted kidneys from cadavers. Why isn't organ transplantation undertaken more often in the United States? Organ donation has not enjoyed the legislative support or the publicity of many other forms of medical treatment. For example, in many European countries one is assumed to be a donor unless one is found to carry a card stating that donation is not desired. In the United States it is quite the opposite: One is presumed to not be interested in donation unless carrying a donor card, and then it is often ignored or the deceased's decision is overturned by family members. Many die each year while waiting on an organ to be donated, many with promising futures who could have lived many more years.

An interesting futuristic procedure is close at hand, that of xenotransplantation. In this procedure, organs are harvested from animals to be transplanted into humans who are waiting for an organ to be donated; in the case of a kidney, the organ would most probably be from a pig. Is this humane? The author would suggest that many millions of people daily eat bacon, ham, and sausage. Also, for those that might snub vital organs transplanted from pigs, haven't we used insulin from pigs for years to treat diabetic patients?

Choosing which waiting patient will get the kidney (or lung or liver) is an interesting topic. Of course, transplantation centers maintain lists of candidates, attempting to match who is most suitable. However, with all things being equal, should the candidate who is youngest or with the most money get the kidney? What about a random drawing for the kidney, or selecting the person that has led the best life? Is a nurse "better" than a teacher or a police officer? What about a professional gambler or a prostitute? This area of thought leads to the field of bioethics, a subset of philosophy. Should the reader be interested, there are many masters' and PhD programs in bioethics.

PERITONEAL DIALYSIS

If a patient experiencing kidney problems cannot find a suitable organ immediately and wishes to have a relatively active lifestyle, peritoneal dialysis may be appropriate. This procedure, because it is done at home, is a measure typically used before the procedure of hemodialysis is undertaken.

For the continuous ambulatory peritoneal dialysis procedure, a catheter is placed in the abdomen of the patient usually 10 to 14 days before dialysis is begun. The dialysis procedure then is as follows:

- Fill: The dialysis fluid enters the patient's peritoneal cavity.
- Dwell: Extra fluid and waste cross the peritoneal membrane into the dialysis fluid.
- Drain: The dialysis fluid is drained and replaced with new fluid.

This procedure may be repeated four times each day, with the fluid staying in the person's abdomen for about 4 hours.

Continuous cycling peritoneal dialysis is much the same as above except that a machine automatically fills and drains the fluid during a 10-hour process while the patient is asleep. These procedures provide approximately 10% efficiency of normal kidneys and do not reverse or treat kidney failure.

HEMODIALYSIS

For hemodialysis, the patient is connected to the dialyzing machine by tubing connected to their blood vessels. The patient's blood leaves the body, going into the filtering dialyzing machine where extra fluid and waste products are removed, and then the filtered blood is returned to the body. This procedure usually lasts about 5 hours and is done three times a week in the outpatient dialysis center while the patient reads or watches television. Side effects may include low blood pressure, muscle cramps, and infections around the catheter site.

PERITONEAL DIALYSIS VERSUS HEMODIALYSIS

Peritoneal dialysis does not require anticoagulants because it is a procedure not using blood vessels. It also does not cause rapid changes in blood pressure. This is a procedure usually chosen by those with an active lifestyle but does require the patient or family members to actively be involved in the use of the equipment.

Hemodialysis is undertaken by skilled healthcare providers. It can be used for patients with abdominal problems or inflammatory bowel disease. As mentioned before, kidney transplants are a better alternative for those fortunate enough to find a suitable donor.

CHAPTER SUMMARY

Kidney failure is an increasingly serious health problem as a direct result of the number of diabetic patients. Though transplantation is the preferred option, this is not always an option due to insufficient donors. Peritoneal or hemodialysis may be used as an option to transplantation or may be the only permanent alternative.

CHAPTER REVIEW

1. What are leading causes of kidney failure?
2. What is the main reason why a patient may not receive a kidney transplant?
3. Are transplanted kidneys a better alternative than dialysis?
4. What can society do to encourage organ donation?
5. What is the difference between peritoneal dialysis and hemodialysis?

Discussion: A friend of yours has been told by her doctor that she could face end-stage renal disease one day if her diabetes is not kept under tight control. Knowing that you are employed in health care, she asks you what this means and what treatments might be available. Please discuss her treatment options with her.

Chapter 25

Home Health Care

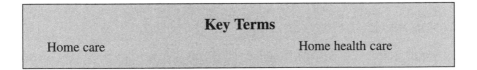

Key Terms

Home care   Home health care

INTRODUCTION

It is generally thought that the elderly population in the United States will more than double to 80 million people between now and the year 2050. Most of those people will probably at one time in their lives be dependent on someone else for all or part of their health care. **Home health care** is designed to meet the growing needs of this increasing segment of the population.

EVOLUTION OF HOME HEALTH CARE

Home health care has evolved from a group of women caring for the ill and elderly in their own homes into one of the fastest growing sectors of the health-care industry due primarily to the passage of Medicare and Medicaid in 1965. Home health care allows a person with special needs to remain in her or his own home rather than to be in institutionalized care or in a long-term nursing home. Though largely focused on the elderly, home health care is available to anyone who may be chronically ill, recovering from surgery, or disabled.

MANY FACETS OF HOME HEALTH CARE

Home health care should not be confused with **home care**. Home health care is more medically oriented toward helping patients recover from injuries or illnesses. Most often home healthcare providers work for independent home health agencies, hospital home health agencies, or public health departments that are licensed by the state. On the other hand, home care usually includes housekeeping services like cooking and cleaning and aiding the patient with daily activities. These home care providers are typically unlicensed.

In addition to physician and skilled nursing care, home health care may include other skilled services; for instance, physical and occupational therapy, speech and language therapy, and medical social services. Care and/or therapy are prescribed and authorized by the patient's doctor and are provided and coordinated by the home health staff of professionals. The staff then reports updates about the patient to the patient's physician. Because health care and technology have advanced, many treatments that could only be done in a hospital before can now be done at home where most patients and their families would probably rather be.

HOME HEALTHCARE AGENCIES

Skilled care is delivered to the patient at home by a variety of licensed healthcare professionals who may be working through governmental agencies such as public health, not-for-profit organizations, or private for-profit home health agencies. With the exception of governmental agencies, all other providers must be licensed in most states and meet regulatory requirements. Any agency participating in Medicare and Medicaid programs must complete certification through a federal program and be monitored for compliance with the certification requirements usually through a federal (Medicare) or a state (Medicaid) office. All home health agencies must comply with rules and regulations in the state in which they operate.

Medicare Guidelines for Finding a Home Healthcare Agency

For Medicare to pay for a home healthcare agency, the agency has to be Medicare-approved (certified), limiting the choice of agencies. A website (www.medicare.gov) provides a link to "Home Health Compare" that allows the user to review home healthcare agencies. It supplies the following information:

- Name, address, and phone number of the agency
- Services offered by the agency (nursing care, occupational therapy, physical therapy, etc.)
- Agency's initial date of Medicare certification
- Type of ownership (for-profit, government, non-profit)
- Quality measure (provides information about how well home health agencies care for their patients and whether the patients' ability to perform daily activities is actually improved or merely maintained)

Patients or family members can also contact the doctor and social worker or simply ask friends and relatives if they have had experience with a particular home healthcare agency. All states have departments of health, aging, and social services, and most communities have senior services that may provide referrals for home healthcare agencies.

HOME HEALTHCARE PROVIDERS

The home healthcare staff assigned to each patient is responsible for teaching the patient and the caregiver (whether it is a paid or informal caregiver such as a family member) how to continue the required care (that may include medication or therapy) for the patient to regain independence or to educate the patient in how to live with the illness or disability.

Providers work intently not only with the patient but with the family, perhaps unlike other healthcare settings where the focus is only on the patient. Providers must be able to accept others and be nonjudgmental even when presented with a completely different value system or cultural background. Because of the closeness in which providers work with their patients, they are in a favorable position to promote good health and possibly can influence the patient and family to alter adverse, unhealthy behaviors.

In addition to the physician, the staff may include a licensed nurse, either a registered or a licensed practical nurse, who provides skilled nursing care that includes administering medications, treating open wounds (i.e., bedsores), providing intravenous therapy, and educating the patient on disease management and prevention.

The physical therapist may instruct the patient on how to get in and out of a wheelchair or bathtub by concentrating on strengthening the lower body. The therapist may help the patient to develop mobility through special exercise and may aid in the recovery from joint replacement surgery.

Whereas physical therapy concentrates on strengthening the muscle groups, occupational therapy focuses on activities of everyday living. Patients with limited ability and mobility are taught to maximize their remaining capabilities through the use of exercises and training to perform daily activities like eating or combing one's hair.

Speech therapists aid the patient in recapturing speech proficiency lost through diseases such as strokes or through an injury. A speech therapist can help patients gain confidence to express themselves through improved speech.

Social workers are a vital part of home health care through providing counseling, assisting patients and their families in locating community resources, and by organizing a variety of services specific to the needs of each patient.

Other members of the home healthcare staff are home health aides who normally assist the patient with walking, getting out of bed, bathing, and dressing;

homemakers who perform household duties such as cleaning, laundry, and meal preparation; and companions who normally provide the importance of friendship. Most states have legislation that requires home healthcare agencies to perform criminal background checks and thoroughly screen all home healthcare providers to prevent any reports of abuse or fraud perpetrated against the elderly or incapacitated individuals.

If directly hiring an individual for home health care (not going through an agency), it becomes more important to screen the person. The ability of the individual to do the job can be determined in an interview in which several questions are asked. It also helps if the interviewer has in mind certain qualifications believed necessary for the healthcare provider to be successful.

METHODS OF PAYMENT

Usually, Medicare is the primary source of payment for home healthcare services, followed by Medicaid. Medicare pays for those who are enrolled in the program and mandates that the following conditions be met:

1. A doctor must authorize home medical care and must format a plan for home health care.
2. The patient must require skilled services such as physical therapy or skilled nursing care.
3. The home healthcare agency must be Medicare-certified.
4. The patient must be homebound, meaning that it would take substantial effort to leave home for any activity apart from medical treatment or short trips, for example, to attend a place of worship.

Skilled nursing and home healthcare aide services are paid for by Medicare for a limited time to each patient, but regular home health care is available for as long as the doctor says the services are required and the patient remains eligible. Home healthcare costs depend on which of the healthcare skilled professionals are required and the length of treatment.

Medicaid is a joint federal–state medical assistance program for low-income people and is controlled by the states. Medicaid, through its program, Medicaid Personal Care Assistance Waiver, provides home healthcare services to older adults and disabled persons. This hands-on care program consists of five basic activities of everyday living: bathing, dressing, eating, transfer, and toileting. The Medicaid Waiver program allows eligibility to a person with restrictions in at least two of those activities who has full Medicaid coverage and is under the continuing care of a physician. Funding from state and local governments and community organizations sometimes pays for needed care when the patient is indigent and other options are not available.

The Veterans Administration and the Older Americans Act can provide financial support for home health care for those meeting the requirements. Workers' compensation provides payment for home health care for an employee who has an illness or injury that occurred from his or her employment, providing that the patient has been established as eligible for workers' compensation benefits and has a licensed physician's authorization. Other sources of funding include commercial and private insurance plans (more companies are providing home healthcare services to their policyholders as an option to more costly institutional care), self-pay, family, and some community organizations.

CHAPTER SUMMARY

Home health care is a much cheaper alternative to traditional institutional care such as long-term care or hospitalization. Both a wide array of providers and options for payment exist to assist many with this form of health care.

CHAPTER REVIEW

1. Who are some of the providers that may be found in a home healthcare setting?
2. What type of patients likely requires home health care?
3. Who may be some of the payers for home health care?
4. What are the advantages of home health care over institutionalized care?
5. Is the need for and provision of home health care likely to increase or decrease during the next 20 years? Why?

Discussion: Your friend's mother had a recent accident and is hospitalized. Her physician has suggested discharge and that home health care be provided as an alternative to her continuing stay in the hospital. What are likely advantages and disadvantages to the physician's suggestion?

Chapter 26

HIV and AIDS Clinics

INTRODUCTION

The disease known as **acquired immunodeficiency syndrome (AIDS)** is not the death sentence it was just a few years ago. People can keep their **human immunodeficiency virus (HIV)**-positive infection from progressing into AIDS and can also extend their life. HIV-positive and AIDS patients may seek help from their physician or may choose to derive health services from a clinic specializing in the case management, treatment, and education of this particular disease. Often, other services such as those for mental health, chemical dependency, and counseling are provided, along with education and support if there is a significant other in the relationship.

SERVICE OFFERED

Typical services in an HIV and AIDS clinic may include but not be limited to the following:

- Anonymous testing of anyone who may believe he or she at risk of exposure
- Prevention of the spread of the illness (condom use and needle exchange programs)

- Ongoing management of chronic conditions
- Treatment of acute health problems
- Complete physical examinations and laboratory testing, including viral burden assays and CD4 counts
- Initiating and monitoring prophylactic therapy for opportunistic infections
- Participating where appropriate in phase IV clinical drug trials
- Referral to support groups
- Health education and risk reduction support
- Legal referrals for wills, durable power of attorney for health care, estate and trust planning, and discrimination issues
- Substance abuse counseling
- Nutritional assessment and nutritional planning
- Treatment of sexually transmitted diseases
- Pelvic examinations and Pap smears
- Family planning
- Religious counseling and referral services

The author recently completed a legal course entitled "HIV and the Law" while working toward an LLM in healthcare law. During the course the instructor mandated that the class visit a non-profit public health clinic such as just described, targeting HIV and AIDS patients. Following this and periodically during the semester, several HIV-positive citizens came to the class as guest speakers, including a gay man, a heterosexual middle-aged woman that had been infected by her husband, and a senior-citizen African-American woman with several grandchildren. The author trusts that those reading this book realize that HIV and AIDS are simply diseases to be treated by healthcare providers while neither passing judgment nor stigmatizing.

CHAPTER SUMMARY

HIV and AIDS are complicated diseases that impact their victims and society harshly. However, they are not the automatic death sentence they were just a few years ago. People can be treated and may live for many years.

CHAPTER REVIEW

1. What services may be expected at an HIV and AIDS healthcare clinic?
2. What services may be expected by the significant others of the patient?
3. What legal services might an HIV or AIDS patient want to receive?

4. What educational messages might the clinic wish to deliver to the general community?
5. What educational messages might the clinic wish to deliver to physicians practicing in the community?

Discussion: Your friend confides in you that he engaged in unsafe sex and doesn't know much about the background of the other person. Your friend wishes to undertake an anonymous HIV test and is not sure where to go. What advice would you give your friend?

Chapter 27

Oncology Centers

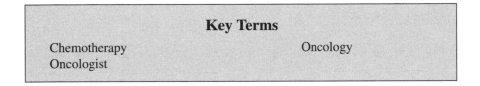

Key Terms

Chemotherapy   Oncology
Oncologist

INTRODUCTION

Heart disease is no longer the leading cause of death in the United States of those under 85; instead it is cancer in its many forms. This is not due to increases in cancer; it is due to advances in the treatment of heart disease and a leveling out of the number of people who use tobacco products.

A WAR ON CANCER?

Many believe that a war on cancer will effectively eradicate the problem, much as deaths from smallpox were reduced when a vaccine was discovered. This is a naive approach, exposing the person as one who simply does not understand the many variations and complications of the disease.

Cancer comes in many forms, such as cancers of the breast, skin, lungs, stomach, blood, and eye. Cancer can be rapidly fatal, as in pancreatic cancer, often giving the patient 6 weeks to perhaps 6 months to live. In other cases the cancer may grow slowly, for example, prostate cancer; the patient most often dies of something else.

Cancer may be part of the patient's blood system and can be treated in hematology centers, or the cancer may be an encapsulated neoplasm and be removed by surgery. It may occur in a lung, and the treatment selected by the physician is a lung transplant (though this is not common as the number of organ donors remains low), or it may be patches on the skin treated with creams, light, or removed through excision or cryogen liquids. Usually more serious forms of cancer are treated by an **oncologist,** a physician specializing in the treatment of cancer, known as **oncology.**

Perhaps a reduction in the number of cancers lies within all of us. Perhaps many cancers can more properly be categorized as "self-inflicted" diseases. In a study reported by *The Economist* in November 2007, the World Cancer Research Fund found that during a 6-year period nine institutes of research, who examined more than a half million publications, discovered 7,000 articles that focused on reducing the risk of cancer. (It should be noted that this research project did not focus on the use of tobacco products; tobacco products have already been clearly linked to one-third of all cancers.) These articles, which are the cutting edge findings of medical and scientific research, were remarkably consistent in demonstrating the following:

- There are known factors that have been shown to reduce the risk of heart disease, such as losing weight and increasing daily exercise. Correctly addressed, these two factors also work to lower the risk of cancer. Even having 5 body mass index points above the healthy range of 21 to 23 is now linked to doubling the risk of colorectal cancer and to doubling the risk of postmenopausal beast cancer.
- Poor choices of food and a lack of exercise are now linked to one-third of all cancers.
- The remaining one-third of all cancers fall into the multifaceted group of genetic predisposition, radiation, environmental pollution, and the use of pesticides, asbestos insulation in older homes, and a host of other reasons.

Thus the message of these studies and research is that society's focus should be on the prevention of the disease in the first place and not on the treatment of the many forms of cancer after it has occurred. However, because about 500,000, people under the age of 85 die each year of cancer, in this chapter we discuss several forms of treatment that many may experience outside of hospital care.

CHEMOTHERAPY

Certain forms of cancer may be reduced or eliminated through the use of **chemotherapy** products. These highly toxic drugs are compounded for each patient by a highly trained specialist working with the use of a ventilated mixing hood. The drugs are usually delivered to the patient intravenously. After the administration of the drug, the patient may often feel very nauseous, weak, and debilitated. This is normal as the toxic chemicals are attempting to kill the cancer.

RADIATION

Patients may receive radiation treatments for their cancer in several different ways. Two examples are:

1. In the form of a focused beam, similar to an x-ray beam, that passes through the vacant area of an otherwise lead shield. The vacant area that allows the beam to pass through has been cut in the exact shape of the targeted tumor.
2. Radioactive material may also be placed within the patient close to the cancer, in the form of radioactive "seeds," as in the treatment of prostate cancer.

SURGERY

Many skin cancers may be treated by freezing the cancer with liquid gases. Still others may be excised through minor surgery in the dermatologist's office. Although most cancer surgery may remain outside the scope of outpatient care, major surgery should still be mentioned as a treatment option. Certain cancers may be in the form of an encapsulated neoplasm and lend themselves to surgical removal. Other cancers may mandate the removal of an organ, such as certain cases of kidney cancer or lung cancer, allowing the removal of a single kidney or lung.

EXPERIMENTAL DRUGS

If other means have been tried, a patient's physician may enroll the patient in an experimental clinical trial. Untried drugs that have been successful in animal studies may help a patient when other treatment modalities have not been successful.

CHAPTER SUMMARY

Cancer is a very complicated disease with many treatment options. Some patients may receive chemotherapy or radiation in an outpatient setting; others may have certain cancers such as skin cancer surgically removed in an office setting; and still others assist medicine and science by being enrolled in experimental clinical trials.

CHAPTER REVIEW

1. Why has the "war" on cancer not been as successful as once hoped?
2. How may a patient be treated with radiation on an outpatient basis?
3. What is chemotherapy and what are likely side effects?
4. What kind of surgery may be undertaken with cancer patients on an outpatient basis?
5. What changes can a person make in his or her lifestyle and habits to eliminate the possibility of acquiring two-thirds of all known cancers?

Discussion: A friend seeks your advice regarding unusual changes he has noticed in several moles. What advice do you give him?

REFERENCE

To avoid the Big C, stay small. *The Economist,* 1 November, 2007

Chapter 28

Long-Term Acute Care

<table>
<tr><td colspan="2" align="center">**Key Terms**</td></tr>
<tr><td>Hospital within a hospital</td><td>Long-term acute care (LTAC)</td></tr>
</table>

INTRODUCTION

Long-term acute care (LTAC) hospitals were fostered in the United States in the early 1980s to fill a gap between standard acute care hospitals and nursing home facilities. There are more than 400 such hospitals now open with many more planned to address the needs of a growing population of patients (mostly elderly) who have prolonged complex medical problems and who cannot be successfully treated in a conventional healthcare facility. The objective of the LTAC facility is to care for the patient while working toward enough medical recovery to transition the patient to his or her home, nursing home, rehabilitation center, or other medical facility.

PATIENT PROFILE

Patients usually come directly from intensive care units of acute care hospitals. These patients are suffering from prolonged serious or critical illnesses and are thought to require specialized services for more than 25 days. Patients most often arrive at the LTAC hospital on a ventilator or other life support due to chronic or acute respiratory disorders. Respiratory failure and pneumonia are diagnoses seen often in these pulmonary management programs. Patients may also be admitted directly from their home, perhaps after suffering a stroke or with congestive heart failure. Other patients may be recovering from major surgeries, catastrophic or acute illnesses, or injuries and may require services such as intravenous therapy

135

or dialysis. LTAC hospitals provide services for patients recuperating from post-surgical wounds or pressure ulcers through a wound care program.

SERVICES PROVIDED

Services provided at an LTAC hospital may include weaning patients off ventilators, focused nursing care and therapy for patients with medically complex issues, and physical, speech, and occupational therapies for those patients who need a wide array of medical rehabilitation. A staff physician is assigned to each patient, providing 24-hour, 7-day-a-week physician coverage. These doctors are usually specialists in pulmonary and critical care (i.e., internal medicine or rehabilitation). Also available are consulting physicians in the areas of cardiology, psychiatry, pain management, head trauma, and surgery. The severity of the LTAC patient's condition also requires that all care providers within the LTAC hospital have advanced evaluation and intervention skills.

Patients are assisted with their dietary needs and preferences by an on-staff dietitian. Some hospitals have private rooms available based on the medical needs of the patient. A case manager is assigned to review with the family or patient his or her status before being admitted to the acute care hospital. They are questioned as to the patient's mental state, ability to manage everyday living, physical capabilities, and so on. The case manager also facilitates communication to the patient and the family regarding the patient's care. In addition, a wide range of services may be provided:

- Hemodialysis
- Laboratory services
- Pharmacy
- Specialty beds
- Social services

HISTORY OF LTAC HOSPITALS

LTAC hospitals were first established as freestanding specialty care hospitals but now are more likely to be a **hospital within a hospital** model. The number of hospital within a hospital–type LTAC facilities has grown significantly in recent years. Under this model, a third-party acute care hospital leases unused space to the LTAC hospital, usually a separate floor of the host acute care hospital. The LTAC hospital is able to operate minus much of the overhead costs of a freestanding LTAC hospital, and it may often contract with the host hospital for ancillary services (i.e., housekeeping, laboratory, food services, etc.) at an agreeable rate, much in the manner of shared services and helping the acute care facility meet its overhead. Federal regulations require that the LTAC hospital have its own governing body independent from that of the host hospital, have a distinct administrative and employee arrangement, and have a separate medical staff. In this structure, most admissions to the LTAC hospital come from the host hospital with the remainder of patients coming from nearby hospitals. Both models offer no other services other than LTAC.

CHAPTER SUMMARY

Acute care hospitals exist to treat those with acute illnesses and to birth babies. LTAC hospitals generally acquire acute care patients that have stayed longer than 25 days or are expected to stay longer than 25 days but who are currently too ill to go home or to a non–acute care setting. Many of these may be ventilator patients. Most LTAC facilities operate within the walls of an acute care hospital but as a distinct and separate entity, more as in a tenant and landlord relationship.

CHAPTER REVIEW

1. What is the difference between an acute care hospital and an LTAC hospital?
2. Where would you physically find most LTAC facilities?
3. What type of patient would you expect to find in an LTAC hospital?
4. How is an LTAC hospital different from a long-term care facility?
5. Why are most LTAC facilities found within an acute care hospital?

Discussion: Your friend's father was recently involved in a severe automobile accident and is on a ventilator. His physician is recommending that he be discharged from an acute care setting and admitted into an LTAC hospital. Your friend asks you what this is and how it works. How do you address the question?

Chapter 29

Adult Day Care

INTRODUCTION

Adult day care centers are sometimes referred to as adult day services or even adult day health services and are one of the fastest growing areas of community-based care. With the quickly escalating elderly population, nearly every part of the country has seen a rise in the number of these facilities during the last 10 years, although these centers date back further than 20 years. An **adult day care center** provides basic day care services to adults with special needs who might otherwise be placed in a nursing home or a personal care residential home—in other words, adults who are either not capable of full-time independent living or who are isolated and lonely. The center usually also provides a respite for care-givers to prevent caregiver burnout and, more importantly, offers a safe environment that creates peace of mind for both the client and the caregiver.

TYPES OF DAY CARE CENTERS

There are three types of adult day care centers:

1. The social services model, which offers social activities, meals, recreation, and a few health-associated services
2. The medical model, which provides more thorough health and therapeutic services in addition to social services for those individuals who are at risk of requiring nursing home care

139

3. Dementia specific, which make available social and health services only to clients who have been diagnosed with dementia

Each of these types may be stand-alone centers or may be located within senior centers, nursing facilities, hospitals, schools, or churches.

CLIENT PROFILE

In an adult day care center, the typical attendee is a senior (probably over 70 years of age) who may be dependent on others because of physical and/or mental disabilities such as Parkinson's disease, stroke, and/or mental illness. Other people may attend the center for any of the following reasons:

- They may be in jeopardy if left at home alone because of working family members
- They require rehabilitation therapy after a hospital stay
- They desire socialization outside the home, preventing social isolation
- They may be a younger person with early-onset Alzheimer's disease or other forms of dementia

A few adult day care centers may require a physical examination conducted by a physician before attending to determine the potential client's abilities and needs. Clients may also be required to be mobile, possibly assisted by a cane, wheelchair, or walker, and may be required to be continent.

SERVICES PROVIDED

Usually, adult day care centers provide standard services and attempt to comply with their respective state or local laws. Typically, services can include:

- Nutritious meals, which may include breakfast, lunch, and/or snacks prepared under the direction of a licensed dietitian to accommodate special diets
- Supervised care in a safe and familiar environment
- Medication administration
- Transportation to and from the center, normally in the form of a handicapped accessible van
- Socialization and peer support
- Fun and educational activities

- Personal care such as hair styling and manicures that are usually optional services brought in by specialists in the community, usually for an added fee
- Individual counseling to aid the client in dealing with anxiety or depression and advice, usually from a visiting social worker, concerning availability of other community services
- Support groups from families and caregivers
- A well-trained and qualified staff (director, nurse, activity director, rehabilitation therapist, etc.) and volunteer workers from a local hospital or from the community

Some "boutique" adult day care centers may provide door-to-door transportation in "luxury" vans, have better meals prepared by a chef, and have a registered nurse on duty.

ACTIVITIES OFFERED

Activities are usually scheduled throughout the day with a focus on the interest of the group, although some activities may be individualized. Popular activities may be singing and music, games that are mentally stimulating such as bingo, fitness in the form of mild exercise, birthday celebrations, group trips (e.g., to museums), and social interaction that may include discussions of books, movies, or current events. Visits from local school children or well-behaved pets are another form of activity that may be welcomed by the center clients. Adult day care centers that are supported by faith-based organizations or church ministries traditionally offer spiritual enrichment activities.

TYPICAL HOURS OF OPERATION AND COSTS

Of course, each adult day care center has its own hours of operation, typically Monday through Friday, 7 a.m. to 6 p.m. Some centers, however, have early drop-off and late pick-up and may have Saturday hours.

Fees for adult day care centers could range from $25 to as much as $100 per day, depending on what services are offered and the geographical region in which the center is located. Obviously, a "boutique" adult day care center in an upscale area would be more expensive. Most facilities charge a sliding fee scale, with those that use the service every day paying less per day than those who infrequently use the service. In addition, meals, transportation, add-on services, and extra activities (e.g., museum trip) may incur additional ancillary costs.

Medicare or most insurance plans do not cover adult day care center costs, but some long-term care insurance policies may provide limited coverage. Some financial assistance may be available through Medicaid if the center is a licensed medical model or "dementia-specific" center and the client meets financial qualifications. The Older Americans Act (Title III) and the Veterans Administration may also provide financial assistance along with area agencies on aging.

Private (philanthropic) or public organizations such as hospital systems and churches also contribute funding, but most adult day care participants are private pay. Either the clients, with their own monetary sources, or family members pay out of pocket. Tax credits may also be available for the care of the elderly.

CLIENT RIGHTS

Participants in an adult day care center should always be ensured of the same rights extended to other adults. These could include the right to (1) be treated as an adult, with respect and dignity; (2) participate in services and activities to the best of their capabilities; (3) engage in programs that enhance learning and growth in ways that develop their interests and talents; (4) maintain their independence; (5) participate if able in developing their own care plan; (6) be cared for with sincere interest and concern; (7) have privacy and confidentiality; (8) be free of physical and mental abuse; and (9) be free of discrimination or reprisal.

TYPICAL LAWS AND REGULATIONS

Not all states require the licensing of adult day care centers unless the facility accepts clients with Medicaid insurance. In states requiring certification or licensing, the agencies usually in charge of state regulations are the state Department of Health or the Department of Social Services. However, if providing medications as a service, the center could be expected to have qualified staff in accordance with state law.

CHAPTER SUMMARY

Adult day care centers have recently become popular as a way of caring for the elderly while two-income earners go to work each day. Day care clients can expect warm meals, activities with others of their age, and medical support for their needs.

CHAPTER REVIEW

1. Who are typical clients in an adult day care center?
2. What services would you expect to find?

3. Who could be expected to pay for adult day care services?
4. What are the alternatives to adult day care services?
5. What laws and regulations could be expected to govern adult day care services?

Discussion: Now that you are in college, your mother is thinking of returning to the workforce. She is concerned that her aging father who has been living with the family may no longer be able to care for himself. What options do you believe your mother may have for his care?

Chapter 30

Geriatric Assessment Clinics and Rheumatology

Key Terms

Arthritis   Gout
Cognitive disorders   Lupus
Fibromyalgia   Rheumatology
Geriatric assessment clinic

INTRODUCTION

As Americans age, more and more elderly people are experiencing confusion, memory loss, dementia, depression, and other chronic medical conditions. A **geriatric assessment clinic** works to improve the life of the elderly by providing a comprehensive evaluation, along with diagnosis and treatment modalities that enable the patient to remain independent for as long as possible. A geriatric assessment of this kind can rule out other physical or psychiatric problems along with medication interactions, allowing an identification of the real cause of most cognitive problems.

ASSESSMENT TEAM

The healthcare team at a geriatric assessment clinic is generally directed by a physician (also the team's director) who is certified in gerontology (the scientific study of aging). Other members of the team are most likely a geriatric nurse, a social worker responsible for any psychosocial evaluations, a consultant in geriatric medicine, and, of course, the patient.

COMMUNITY SERVICES FOR GERIATRIC PATIENTS

A plan for continuity of care is based on the findings of the multidisciplinary team. The patient is often referred to specialty geriatric services in the community:

- Podiatric care: Periodic examination of the patient's feet for signs of arthritis and comprised circulation, especially in diabetic patients, is very important. In addition, problems for elders could be foot care for bunions, calluses, and in-grown toenails. Podiatric care is synonymous with relieving symptoms of foot problems and keeping older persons mobile and active.
- Diabetes care: Aging is a key risk factor in the progression of diabetes. Diabetes in the elderly often is undiagnosed and untreated. Clinics that specialize in endocrinology and diabetes care provide nutritional management, exercise, and pharmacological therapy to ensure the optimization of blood glucose control for the older patient.
- Urinary incontinence: This is a major concern for elderly patients not only because of physiological effects but because of the psychological effects. Due to childbirth and/or obesity, which result in the loss of pelvic muscles, women can be more prone to urinary incontinence. Incontinence that cannot be cured can be treated by having the patient wear absorbent pads or adult diapers.
- **Cognitive disorders**: Memory loss and other cognitive changes are among the most common problems seen in a geriatric assessment clinic. This can result in a referral to a specialist for treatment. Alzheimer's disease, a form of dementia, is among the most common reasons for people to be in long-term care facilities. The disease affects sections of the brain that control thought, memory, and language. No one knows the cause of Alzheimer's disease, and there is no known cure, although there are newer drugs that may help to prevent the disease from progressing in some patients.
- Physical rehabilitation: Once more, the focus is on making the elderly patient mobile and functionally independent, preferably in his or her own home. Because the elderly are usually more prone to falls resulting in broken bones, physical rehabilitation is imperative to resuming the older patient's autonomy and well-being. Exercises can include swimming or other activities as simple as tai chi. Getting the patient actively involved in rehabilitation after a fall can greatly improve his or her quality of life. Caregivers and family members can be made aware of fall prevention methods. Often, improving the patient's environment to eliminate obstacles that could cause another fall is as simple as supplying correct walking aids, for example, walkers or canes.

Because most people will reach geriatric age, it is important that everyone should learn as much as possible about aging to anticipate this period and to stay healthy. Aging is a natural process. Everyone should aspire to lead energetic, useful lives with autonomy. No one wants to need care, but if it is necessary, the geriatric assessment clinic may be helpful.

RHEUMATOLOGY

Rheumatology is the practice of diagnosing and treating chronic rheumatic diseases. All ages, genders, and races are affected by these diseases that are sometimes complex. Often, a multidisciplinary team is required to focus on preventing disability by educating the patient in how best to cope, take medications, and improve the quality of life through rehabilitation.

Rheumatologist

A rheumatologist is a doctor who has completed an internal medicine residency and a fellowship program in rheumatology, becoming board certified. Rheumatologists usually maintain a private practice or clinic in which they provide care. They also work in hospitals, outpatient clinics, and managed care practices. Patients are most often referred to a rheumatologist by their primary care physician who diagnoses rheumatic disease and understands that the patient needs more advanced care.

During a consultation with a rheumatologist, the patient can expect many questions regarding symptoms and pain, daily activities, stress level, and family history. During the examination, the rheumatologist will ask more questions as he or she examines the patient for visible signs of rheumatic diseases. Some of the indicators may be sensitivity, swelling, redness, and inflammation. The rheumatologist may order further diagnostic tests to formulate a diagnosis and the best treatment approach:

- Blood tests: These are not definitive in the diagnosis of rheumatic diseases when used alone but can be of valuable assistance. Blood tests are also used to monitor the effectiveness of treatment of rheumatic diseases and to detect problems in the liver or kidney.
- Joint fluid analysis: This may be used to determine causes of joint pain, swelling, and inflammation.
- Thermal imaging studies: These may be used to detect early arthritis to begin appropriate treatment.

Upon completion of the consultation and examination, the rheumatologist may instruct the patient in the management of the rheumatic disease so as to continue a useful and productive life. Topics of discussion can be nutrition, exercise, weight control, and physical therapy, all of which require patient involvement to ensure a good outcome during treatment.

Many communities have rheumatoid support groups. The physician can refer the patient to other healthcare providers such as nurses, social workers, orthopedic surgeons, and pharmacists. The rheumatologist can explain the importance of being optimistic and coping with and controlling the disease; this can assist in fostering a positive outcome.

Arthritis and Other Related Rheumatic Conditions

Arthritis literally means joint inflammation. Arthritis is one of many autoimmune diseases that can cause pain in joints. Arthritis, left untreated, may become debilitating, causing permanent damage in the joints and bones. The two most common types of arthritis are osteoarthritis (damage to joint cartilage that has developed gradually due to "wear and tear," causing pain and partial range of motion) and rheumatoid arthritis (an inflammatory type of arthritis that progresses gradually causing joint pain, swelling, and stiffness). Though there is no known cure for these chronic conditions, heredity is thought to play a role in their development. Certain environmental factors like smoking are also believed to increase the risk of developing rheumatoid arthritis.

Fibromyalgia is a painful rheumatic condition distinguished by muscle pain in areas of the body when pressure is applied. Fibromyalgia is a chronic disease but is neither progressive nor life threatening. Diagnosis is centered on patient symptoms and physical examination and may reveal additional symptoms such as headaches, restless leg syndrome, anxiety and depression, and hypersensitivity to temperature. Symptoms can be relieved by reducing stress, acquiring the proper amount of sleep, regular exercise, and a proper diet. Choices of medications that may help to reduce pain and improve sleep include analgesics, antidepressants, and muscle relaxants, which primarily treat the symptoms. Alternative medicine such as chiropractic care, massage therapy, and acupuncture may also relieve the pain of fibromyalgia.

King Henry VIII is reported to have possibly suffered from gout due to his obesity. **Gout** is a painful form of arthritis that normally affects the feet and especially the big toe, causing painful swelling. Gout is caused by excess uric acid that builds up in the body, creating crystals that deposit in various joints. Once a diagnosis is made confirming gout, treatment usually consists of nonsteroidal anti-inflammatory drugs that work to decrease inflammation and pain in joints.

Patients unable to take those drugs because of other medical conditions such as ulcers are sometimes given prescriptions for corticosteroids (a class of steroid hormones to reduce inflammation). A change in diet, elimination of alcohol, and a weight loss program are encouraged to enable the patient to manage this chronic disease.

Lupus is an autoimmune disease, certainly not confined to the elderly, that mainly involves the skin, joints, and heart; it may also create mental health problems. Symptoms depend on what part of the body is affected by this rheumatic condition. Chronic fatigue, joint pain (arthritis), and skin rashes are common symptoms of lupus. Joint and muscle pain are often the first signs of lupus, causing redness and swelling mainly in the hand joints, wrists, elbows, and ankles. Most victims of lupus experience a skin rash on the arms, hands, face, and neck or may have sores on the mouth. They also go through bouts of sensitivity to light (especially sunlight), headaches, fever, swollen glands, and hair loss, which is usually not permanent. Treatment for lupus depends on how debilitating the disease has become. As the disease changes, either improving or becoming worse, treatment plans change. Self-care and medication along with education about the disease help the patient and rheumatologist develop an effective treatment plan. Flare-ups should be treated quickly to diminish body organ damage. Treatment might include:

- Avoiding the sun and applying sunscreen
- Spreading corticosteroid cream over rashes
- Taking nonsteroidal anti-inflammatory drugs
- Regular exercise and a good diet
- Getting plenty of rest
- Eliminating smoking

Like other rheumatic diseases, the treatment of lupus can be aided through a positive attitude and a support group made up of family and friends. In addition, a multidisciplinary healthcare team will enable the affected patient to live a more productive life.

CHAPTER SUMMARY

Geriatric assessment clinics may be very valuable in pinpointing disease or potential disease among the elderly. Rheumatism and related forms of arthritis such as fibromyalgia, gout, or lupus may be very debilitating diseases among the elderly, requiring specialists in medicine.

CHAPTER REVIEW

1. What is rheumatism and who should one see for diagnosis and treatment?
2. What is gout and what are suggested treatments?
3. What is lupus and what is the best course of treatment?
4. What is fibromyalgia and how is it treated?
5. What forms of examinations would you expect to find in a geriatric assessment center?

Discussion: Your friend has been complaining to you of chronic fatigue and now has a skin rash on his hands and arms. You suspect an onset of lupus. With whom would you suggest he make an appointment?

Chapter 31

Long-Term Care

Key Terms

Domiciliary care   Long-term care

Intermediate care   Retirement village

INTRODUCTION

Long-term care was once simply thought of as a nursing home where many elderly went when they could no longer care for themselves or their relatives could not provide care. This is no longer the case, with long-term care being delivered in a variety of settings and having a much higher level of acceptability. The chapter begins with the simplest variety and works toward the more complex.

A THREE-TIERED STEPPING STONE PROCESS

The Independent Retirement Village

Although it may seem odd to think of a **retirement village** as providing long-term care, it is seen increasingly as the entry point for older citizens as they move toward needing greater care. Often, couples will sell a larger home when they have an "empty nest" and purchase or lease, in a retirement community, a smaller garden-style home or apartment that is easier to maintain. This can have the added advantage of being on a single level, eliminating the hazards and inconvenience of stairs. These units are called "independent living units" or "self-care units" in which care is provided at a very low level. This may be in a simple form such as the provision by the village of garden and lawn maintenance. Many seniors look forward to golfing and socializing with their friends in areas that provide optimal year-round weather. In many cases electric golf carts are the primary transportation to and from conveniently located stores within the retirement village. Many residents have their own automobiles and have the ability to come and go at will. Most all communities provide either a garage or carport. For those who do not drive, villages provide van transportation to shopping and appointments and provide buses for tours and trips. Most villagers engage in social activities (indoor and out) provided by the community and may even have rental units for family members or friends to stay for short periods of time.

Retirement villages may host special services such as enhanced security, visiting home health care, and "Meals-on-Wheels" that provide added convenience to their residents. It is not unusual for community purchased services to include weekly housecleaning and maintenance, bill paying, and sometimes even daily reminders to take medicines. The couple, or often the surviving spouse, may tire of cooking or may be unable to cook for themselves. Many retirement village residents opt, through higher fees, to join others in a communal dining hall. Professional cooks prepare cafeteria-style meals that are served during fixed times, allowing residents the convenience of not having to shop, cook, and clean up. The meals are generally more balanced and nutritious and may be tailored to unique dietary needs.

Retirement village housing can be single residences, apartment buildings, manufactured homes, or perhaps townhouses. They can be bought or leased. Residents as a rule have sold their primary home to buy or lease into the housing. These villages are often owned by or associated with prominent medical centers and are generally located near hospitals and doctors' offices, making them convenient for the residents to seek medical care. In these retirement communities, seniors are not dependent on their families for their care but instead retain their independence with a worry-free lifestyle.

Intermediate Care or Assisted Living

A day will come when the resident of the retirement village may need additional help with everyday tasks but does not require nursing facility services such as extensive medical or nursing care. The move is then made from the "independent unit" into an "assisted living unit" or "supported care unit" that offers care at a higher level and usually includes a variety of personal services. This is known as **intermediate care**. He or she may need someone to help with dressing, bathing, or perhaps even eating. A nursing staff is on duty 24 hours a day to assist with emergencies or medical problems. The person is given assistance with hygiene and medication services, allowing continued autonomy while having periods of confusion or experiencing memory problems. Housekeeping is provided in these units. In addition, residents are provided 24-hour security services, independence, dignity, and privacy as desired. Not an alternative to a nursing home, assisted living is an intermediate level of long-term care.

Assisted living residences can be high-rise apartments or residential-type homes; they can be private or semiprivate; the units may be furnished or unfurnished, which allows the resident to bring his or her cherished belongings; and they can be equipped with a kitchen or provided with group dining facilities. Most residents pay with their own personal funds, usually from savings; a smaller percentage pay with Supplementary Security Income (SSI), whereas an even smaller percentage pay with family assistance funds. Long-term care insurance policies provide funding, but few seniors have policies. Medicare does not pay for assisted living except for certain services covered by SSI. There is a move by some states to have the option to pay for assisted living under Medicaid services for people who are not able to afford the expenses themselves.

Most assisted living communities provide many activities such as exercise classes, church services, craft sessions, and movies. There may be large-screen televisions located in lounge areas where many of the residents gather for companionship. Many facilities also allow residents to keep domestic animals, realizing the important connection people have with their pets.

The promotion of physical and social well-being makes assisted living quite popular with seniors and their families. Assisted living allows seniors to live as independently as possible for as long as possible before the transition to full nursing home care.

Full Care

When the resident of the assisted living community can no longer care for himself or herself or has reached a stage where the caregiver can no longer provide assisted care, the person may then transition into an "around-the-clock" skilled nursing facility or nursing home. In addition to medical care, the resident may need physical, speech, or occupational therapy. A social worker may be on staff to assist the new resident in acclimating to his or her new surroundings, to locate funding, and to help the family adjust to the change. Family involvement is encouraged to prevent the resident from feeling abandoned, helpless, and isolated from family members. In this environment, the resident may eat in the company of other residents but has no responsibility for cleaning, medical care, shopping, or responsibilities of everyday living. Units often contain a bed or sometimes two beds, with some facilities encouraging residents to bring familiar items from home. Some nursing homes allow couples to share a room; some even allow pets. Patients can expect visits several times a day from a nurse aide who assists them in hygiene, dressing, and, at times, eating. For recreation, the individual may walk or be rolled in a wheelchair to an activity room for bingo, television, or group social activities. In good weather, he or she may be accompanied outdoors by a nurse aide. For those who are physically able, there may be occasional accompanied excursions to local museums, malls, or sports events to provide added entertainment. Certainly, the residents have enhanced medical care provided by a physician who visits at least weekly.

It may be surprising to learn that not all residents of long-term care facilities are elderly. Often, younger citizens who may be physically or mentally challenged reside in the facility, usually when families are unable to provide daily care. Some facilities offer areas designed specifically for meeting the needs of people with dementia or Alzheimer's disease. Doors are equipped with alarms requiring a code to exit, thus keeping the residents from wandering. Needing chronic care, these individuals find medical care and have assistance with issues of everyday living.

Methods of payment can range from Medicare (pays only for medically necessary skilled nursing facility or home health care), Medicaid (a state and federal government program that pays for certain health services and nursing home care for older people with low incomes and limited assets), private pay (personal savings or family funds), or long-term care insurance (purchased from a private insurance company in the form of a policy). In addition, funds can be derived from other sources such as reverse mortgages (a special type of home loan that allows the homeowner to convert a portion of the equity of his or her home into cash), a life insurance policy settlement (when one sells a life insurance policy for its present value), and viatical settlements (the selling of a life insurance policy to a third party for a portion of the full face value). An alternate financial resource may be the Veterans Administration, which maintains its own skilled nursing facilities (**domiciliary care**) in some areas of the country.

TRENDS IN LONG-TERM CARE

Most experts agree that the long-term care market will increase as the baby boom generation ages. There are a host of reasons, among which are increased natural life spans, enhanced medical care that saves and prolongs life, awareness of health issues such as improved nutrition and the elimination of tobacco products, and an enhanced affluence among the elderly that can include those who purchased long-term care insurance products earlier in life.

Problems in the long-term care industry are significant. With the increasing number of elderly, the supply of long-term care beds is probably not adequate. In part this may be due to states not fostering the creation of more beds, knowing that their Medicaid expenditures would have to increase.

Nursing homes have too often been the source of abuse of the elderly, driven in part by thin profit margins and low wages to caregivers. This has, in turn, driven investigations, tighter regulations, and the licensing of many of the staff including the nursing home administrator. (Note: Although hospitals are much more complex organizations, hospital administrators are not required by any state to be licensed.)

Recently, Vermont enacted legislation aimed at discouraging long-term care facilities and enhancing care provided by family members. Realizing that someone must stay home with the elder relative yet at the same time the household must have two breadwinners, the state authorized payment to the caregiver who stays at home. When medical care is needed that is more complex than the caregiver's ability to administer (e.g., intravenous lines), a home health specialist drops by to provide care. Not having to leave the house and thus providing care, the second paycheck is given to the household in lieu of Medicaid payments going to the long-term care facility, a win–win situation.

CHAPTER SUMMARY

America is an aging population that will have increasing issues with providing long-term care for its citizens. Long-term care may come in a gradual package, with the recipient moving from an autonomous form of retirement village into an assisted living arrangement and then transitioning into a full care arrangement. Because of a history of abuse, the long-term care industry is heavily regulated.

CHAPTER REVIEW

1. What are some forms of payment for long-term care?
2. Describe the three tiers that may take place as the recipient of care ages and is less able to care for him-or herself.
3. What are some of the problems of aging that most can expect to experience?
4. Are all patients residing in a long-term care facility elderly? If not, what type of healthcare challenges might the patient experience?
5. Why are nursing homes usually more regulated than hospitals?

Discussion: Your 70-year-old grandparents have decided to move from their three-story house where they have a constant fear of falling down the stairs. What alternatives could you suggest for them to explore?

Chapter 32

Hospice and Palliative Care

INTRODUCTION

Hospice care is a concept of care; it should not be thought of as a place of care. The focus is on quality of life rather than the remaining quantity of life. Besides health care, psychological care, emotional care, spiritual care, and social services are emphasized. The hospice program strives to affirm life and regards the time during the end of life as a normal part and process of life. The hospice team strives to see the uniqueness and special requirements of each individual and family, so as to be sensitive and responsive.

Hospice programs assist the terminally ill to live their remaining days with dignity. They also assist in training the person's family or other loved ones with how to administer drugs or other essential healthcare support. Hospice beds may be part of an inpatient program in a hospital or long-term care facility, or the person may receive hospice care in his or her own home by way of visiting nurses or hospice volunteers.

THE HOSPICE TEAM

Hospice caregivers can be composed of the following:

- The physician, whose role is to make the diagnosis of the patient having less than 6 months to live and to prescribe pain medications

157

- Nurses, who write and supervise the overall care plan
- Home health aides, who deliver care, which can be 7 days a week
- Clergy or other spiritual leaders and counselors (rabbi, mullah, priest, minister, etc.)
- Social workers, who may advise the recipient of available community services, both health care and financial
- Hospice volunteers that work to provide emotional support and invaluable simple things such as running errands to assist the patient and the family. These very important people may also provide "respite" care, which provides family members a break from the emotional strain and can provide new and understanding companionship to the patient.
- Occupational, physical, and/or speech therapists if needed
- Attorneys, who provide expertise in writing an estate plan, a will, a **living will**, **advanced directives**, or other end-of-life documents

IS HOSPICE CARE APPROPRIATE FOR EVERYONE?

The choice of hospice care is deeply personal. This can be driven by the patient's personal philosophy of life, spiritual beliefs or value system, age and physical condition, and the concerns of his or her family members. For example, many people when being told they have a terminal medical condition may wish to explore every extraordinary means and remedy to extend their life, grasping at mainstream and non-mainstream medicine such as herbal or folk remedies. They may request that their physician quickly enroll them in clinical trials for yet unproven medications. On the other hand, others may simply think, "Hey, I've lived a good life, I've known that this time comes for everyone, and I would prefer to spend the time remaining putting my affairs in order, saying goodbye, and dying as painlessly as possible and with dignity."

CHOOSING A HOSPICE CENTER OR YOUR HOME

When a person chooses to accept hospice care, he or she may elect to go to a hospice center (provided their city has such a center or has a hospital providing hospice beds) or the individual may elect to receive hospice care in his or her own home, as 90% of hospice patients choose.

A formal hospice center may provide a homelike environment with registered nurses that provide assessment and supervision. Meals are prepared, linen is changed, and many spiritual advisors are available for patients. However, it is still not the patient's own home, which most patients prefer.

Hospice care in someone's own home is the majority choice, though it may be taxing on family members. In this setting a home health aide may drop by daily to check on the patient and to deliver and assist with pain medications.

Advances in the acceptance of pain medications have come a long way in recent years. It wasn't long ago that the predominant and ridiculous thought was, "Don't give medications too long or too strong, the patient may become addicted." Current thinking is more along the line of "the patient has the right to dignity and to be pain free."

PALLIATIVE CARE

Palliative care is the treatment of suffering or symptoms of a serious illness that is not able to be cured. Even though life-prolonging therapies are incorporated, the control of symptoms is emphasized to enhance the patient's quality of like. The patient's goals and values are respected, and the patient's preferences for care may change as the condition and disease worsens.

When significant life-prolonging therapy is no longer an option, it may become appropriate to discuss comfort and palliative care and less aggressive acute care. Issues of resuscitation and artificial ventilation are important but may not be the sole issues. Invasive tests, chemotherapy, dialysis, and surgery become less important and, instead, controlling pain and other symptoms come to the forefront of discussion.

Palliative care may be provided to patients at all stages of their illness. Hospice care, on the other hand, is usually prescribed and limited to patients when their viability for life is thought to be 6 months or less. In fact, many inpatient hospices only accept patients with 3 months or less to live.

Trying to predict the prognosis of a terminally ill patient can be very inexact. Many physicians err on the side of waiting too long; sometimes a patient is certified for hospice care and then dies within a week or 2. On the other hand, other patients outlive the 6-month estimate. These poor estimates in part can be due to the lack of eagerness of a physician or patient to undertake further, complex, evaluative tests. Invasive tests and imaging may be offered; however, most programs focus as much as possible on comfort, relief of pain, nausea, and respiratory distress. When necessary, testing is limited to non-invasive testing. There is also an emphasis on psychological and spiritual assistance for both the patient and his or her loved ones.

CHAPTER SUMMARY

Hospice care is directed toward the terminally ill patient. It may be provided in the patient's own home or in an actual institution. The practice of hospice care focuses on the control of pain and in making the patient comfortable, rather than racing to find a cure for his or her illness. End-of-life documents and a **durable power of attorney for healthcare decisions** are usually a part of the hospice program.

CHAPTER REVIEW

1. What healthcare resources are available in your community for end-of-life care? How did you find these services?
2. What financial services are available for end-of-life care? What if the patient is uninsured?
3. What are your state and local laws regarding end-of-life decisions? In the author's experience, these vary widely from state to state. As an example, note the vast difference in death and dying laws between the state of Oklahoma and the state of Oregon.
4. Are there attorneys in your area that practice in the area of healthcare and end-of-life issues? This area of legal practice can be very different from the usual drafting of wills, estate planning, and estate taxes and trusts. This area of practice focuses more on an in-depth understanding of health insurance coverage (experimental drugs and procedures), advanced directives, living wills, durable power of attorney for healthcare decisions, and the rights of survivorship of non-married partners.
5. Why is it difficult to know when to refer patients for hospice care?

Discussion: Your friend has been diagnosed with pancreatic cancer. She seeks your advice because she understands that treatment options may be extremely limited. What options can you suggest for her?

Appendix A

Glossary

Acquired immunodeficiency syndrome (AIDS). A person who tests positive for human immunodeficiency virus can be diagnosed with AIDS when a laboratory test shows that his or her immune system is severely weakened by the virus or when he or she develops at least 1 of about 25 different opportunistic infections.

Acne. A common skin inflammation usually treated with topical or oral medications. There may be a genetic predisposition and it may occur many times, usually during the teen years.

Acute care. Hospital inpatient treatment of 25 days or less.

Adult day care center. Community-based care that provides basic day care services to adults with special needs who might otherwise be placed in a nursing home or a personal care residential home.

Advanced directives. These medical directives allow a person to name his or her treatment preferences as well as another person to make medical decisions on his or her behalf. In most states there are three categories of advanced directives: a living will, a durable power of attorney for healthcare decisions, and a healthcare proxy.

Allergies. Over-reaction to usually harmless substances that the immune system determines are harmful, even when they are not.

Allopathic doctor. Designation for a medical doctor or MD.

American College of Healthcare Executives (ACHE). One North Franklin Street, Chicago, Illinois 60606. Formed in 1933. Professional society for healthcare managers and executives. It was formerly called the American College of Hospital Administrators (ACHA). The name was changed in 1985.

Ancillary services. Therapeutic or diagnostic services provided by specific hospital departments (other than nursing services) including but not limited to imaging, laboratories, and physical therapy. Other ancillary services include but are not limited to respiratory therapy, electroencephalography, other forms of rehabilitative medicine, and pharmacy.

Angiography. Also known as arteriography. A test comprised of x-rays and dye to view the arteries in various parts of the body, including the heart, brain, and lungs.

Art therapy. A form of therapy that may include drawing, painting, music, or dance to help a patient to express his or her feelings or thoughts and to increase self-awareness or to cope with traumatic experiences to facilitate positive change.

Arthritis. Literally means joint inflammation. This is usually an autoimmune disease that manifests itself by causing pain in joints.

Assisted reproduction technology (ART). A medical therapy used to increase the possibility of conception. In vitro fertilization and embryo transfer are two procedures of ART.

Asthma. A disease that affects the lungs that may cause repeated episodes of wheezing, breathlessness, tightness of chest, and coughing. If the asthma attack is severe, it can be quite disabling or may cause death. Asthma can be controlled with medication by recognizing the hazards to either prevent or minimize them.

Audiologist. A health provider who diagnoses and treats hearing, ear, or balance-related ear problems.

Average length of stay. The average number of days inpatients remain in a hospital or other health facility from date of admission to date of discharge.

Back office. In the medical practitioner's office, refers to the measurements area, laboratory, imaging, examination rooms, and the physician's office.

Behavior therapy. This is a type of therapy that enables individuals to overcome anxiety, fear, or discomfort usually through a system of rewards or reinforcement of positive behavior.

Bioethics. This refers to the beliefs in rights and wrongs of healthcare procedures and the controversy that often surrounds them. Two examples are (1) the fertilization of excess embryos that may result in eliminating some of the embryos and (2) making the best decision as to who is the recipient of an organ transplant.

Body mass index (BMI). A measurement of height and weight that is used in conjunction with a chart to determine the normal range of an individual's weight.

Bone densitometry. A relatively safe, noninvasive, radiological test used to measure the bone's mineral content and therefore the risk of fracture.

Centers for Disease Control and Prevention (CDC). An agency of the federal Department of Health and Human Services that works to protect public health and safety by providing investigations and information in the prevention and control of disease.

Certified nurse practitioner. A registered nurse with a master's degree and additional training in the diagnosis and treatment of common health problems.

Certified registered nurse anesthetists (CRNAs). Advanced practice nurses who are allowed to administer anesthesia independently or, in some states, under the supervision of a physically available anesthesiologist.

Chemotherapy. Highly toxic drugs that are compounded for a patient in an attempt to destroy cancerous cells.

Chiropractor. A practitioner in the field of chiropractic care, a complementary and alternative healthcare profession that focuses on treating patients with drug-free, non-surgical, hands-on therapy called manipulation or adjustment.

Cognitive disorders. Diseases (Alzheimer's and other dementias) that affect sections of the brain that control thought, memory, and language.

Colonoscopy. An endoscopy procedure used in the diagnosis of colorectal cancer that is normally performed in an outpatient surgicenter.

Computed tomography (CT). Computed tomography, also called computed axial tomography, uses x-rays and high-speed computers to allow enhanced images of the human body that would be impossible with ordinary x-ray procedures.

Convenience clinics. Urgent care centers that are normally found in urban neighborhoods, in retail shopping centers, or in freestanding clinic buildings that are convenient and easy to locate, demand reduced waiting times, and are less expensive.

Dental assistant. A dental office employee who carries out duties with more emphasis on patient care, office, and laboratory duties.

Dental hygienist. A dental office employee who cleans teeth, takes x-rays, takes measurements, and prepares impressions for partials to replace missing teeth.

Dental laboratory technician. The person in dentistry responsible for constructing dental prosthetics such as bridges and crowns. Dental laboratory technicians work with dentists in the manufacture of complete or partial dentures and with orthodontists in making orthodontic appliances such as braces and retainers.

Dentist. A licensed doctor who has graduated from an accredited dental school, usually a 4-year undertaking after 4 years of college.

Dermatologist. One who practices the medical science of dermatology, the pathology and physiology of the skin, hair, and nails.

Dermatology. The medical science dealing with the diagnosis and treatment of the nails, hair, and skin.

Direct access testing (DAT). Medical testing that allows the patient or consumer to access a laboratory and the results without having to consult or even contact a physician.

Dispensing optician. One who fits eyeglasses or contact lenses.

Domiciliary care. Care for the aged veteran, similar to long-term care, provided in a Veterans' Administration setting.

Drawing stations. Medical laboratories that specialize in convenient and quick acquisition of medical specimens.

Durable power of attorney for healthcare decisions. A type of advance directive that allows a person the authority to make decisions in health-related matters for another person who may be incapacitated.

Eczema. A common skin inflammation usually noted by redness and itching, progressing to bumps, thickening of the skin, and then scaling of the skin.

Electroencephalography (EEG). A procedure used to measure the brain's electrical signals. This is useful in diagnosing epilepsy, brain tumors, strokes, and other neurological abnormalities relating to the brain.

Electrocardiography (ECG). A cardiac procedure used in cardiac care to diagnose irregularities in heart action. It records changes in electrical current during a heartbeat, providing an important source of medical diagnostic information.

Electromyography (EMG). A procedure to measure the electrical activity of muscles at rest to find diseases that may damage muscle tissue or nerves.

Embryo. The fetal human product of conception from implantation through the eighth week of development.

Endodontist. A dental specialist who specializes in root canal therapy.

Endoscopy. A visual examination of interior parts of the body with use of an endoscope.

Environmental Protection Agency. An agency of the federal government that has the responsibility of protecting and safeguarding the environment.

Fibromyalgia. A painful rheumatic chronic condition distinguished by muscle pain in exact areas of the body when pressure is applied.

Fluoroscopy. Technique used to view the body structure by sending x-rays through the body part to be examined and then observing the images portrayed on a screen.

Food and Drug Administration. An agency of the U.S. Department of Health and Human Services that is responsible for the safe regulation of most foods, drugs, medical devices, and other products.

Front office. The area of a medical practitioner's office that includes waiting and reception, intake coordinator, appointments, billing, insurance verification, and sometimes a practice manager.

Gamete intrafallopian transfer. A medical procedure that transfers unfertilized eggs and sperm into a woman's fallopian tubes by use of a laparoscope. Small incisions are usually placed in the abdomen, thereby allowing in vivo fertilization rather than in vitro fertilization.

Gastric banding. Restrictive weight loss surgery for obese patients with a body mass index of 40 or greater.

Genetic predisposition. An inherited increase in the susceptibility of developing a particular disease by having certain genes that predispose one to the disease.

Geriatric assessment clinic. A clinic that works to improve the life of the elderly by providing a comprehensive evaluation, along with diagnosis and treatment proposals that enable the patient to remain independent for as long as possible.

Gout. A painful form of arthritis that normally affects the feet and especially the big toe, causing painful swelling.

Health Insurance Portability and Accountability Act (HIPAA). This federal act, passed in 1996, ensures portability of health insurance, adds enforcement to healthcare fraud and abuse, enforces standards for health care, and guarantees security and privacy of health information.

Health maintenance organization. A type of third-party payer plan. There are several types but two common forms are (1) the group model, where health maintenance organizations contract with several group practices and share the risk of the venture with the physicians, and (2) a model where all of the physicians, offices, and equipment are owned and managed by a company that members subscribe to for health care.

Hemodialysis. An invasive procedure that mechanically uses filters to exclude wastes from the body and blood. Usually, patients undertake the procedure 3 times a week for about 5 hours each session.

Home care. A system of housekeeping services such as cooking and cleaning to aid a patient with daily activities in his or her own home.

Home diagnostic tests. An inexpensive and convenient alternative to a doctor's office visit for testing of such things as cholesterol, blood glucose, the presence of illicit drugs, or pregnancy.

Home health care. A healthcare system that allows a person with special needs (e.g., chronically ill and/or elderly) to remain in his or her own home, with health care delivered by a nurse or other caregiver, rather than to be in institutionalized care or in a long-term nursing home.

Hospice care. A concept of care that focuses on pain management and quality of life issues rather than the remaining quantity of life.

Hospital. An institution producing medical and health care every day around the clock. Its primary function is to provide inpatient and outpatient services, including diagnostic and therapeutic services, for a variety of medical and surgical conditions. Some also provide emergency care. Hospitals can be teaching or non-teaching, specialty or non-specialty (psychiatric, general, etc.), proprietary (for profit) or not-for-profit (government, local, private) entities. Most hospitals in the United States are short-term, acute-care, general, and non-profit.

Hospital within a hospital. A long-term acute-care hospital that operates within an acute-care hospital.

Human immunodeficiency virus (HIV). HIV destroys white blood cells called CD4+ T cells. These cells are critical to the normal function of the human immune system, which defends the body against illness. HIV infections often damage a person's immune system and can progress to acquired immunodeficiency syndrome.

Imaging. Medical procedures and techniques used to view internal images of the body to assist in diagnosing and treating the disease.

Immunologist. A medical doctor specialist who is trained in the diagnosis and treatment of allergic diseases and asthma. This physician may treat other diseases of the immune system and may also be referred to as an allergist.

Intermediate care. Also called "assisted living care" or "supported care," this is health care that is between "independent care" and extensive nursing services.

In vitro fertilization (IVF). The joining of a man's sperm and a woman's egg outside the womb in a laboratory dish, test tube, or beaker. In vitro means "outside the body," and fertilization means the sperm has entered the egg.

In vivo fertilization. The joining of a man's sperm and a woman's egg inside the womb rather than artificially outside the womb.

Laparoscopic surgery. A surgical procedure within the abdomen or pelvic cavities using a laparoscope.

LASIK surgery. A surgical procedure using a laser to reshape the eye with the purpose of improving vision without the use of eyeglasses.

Living will. A written document that specifies what types of medical treatment are desired.

Long-term acute care (LTAC). Designed to fill the gap between standard acute care hospitals and nursing home facilities for patients who have prolonged, complex medical problems. These patients need acute care but also long-term care and usually stay longer than 25 days.

Long-term care. Usually, care that is provided in a skilled nursing facility or nursing home.

Lupus. An autoimmune disease that mainly involves the skin, joints, and the heart and may cause certain mental health problems.

Magnetic resonance imaging (MRI). A diagnostic procedure using large magnets and radio signals to produce images of a patient's anatomical structures.

Mammography. A procedure that uses special x-ray images of the breasts as a screen for cancer.

Medicaid. A largely federally funded program but administered by each state to provide health care for the poor of the state.

Medical Group Management Association (MGMA). An organization for healthcare professionals employed in the management of medical group practice.

Medicare. Title XVIII of the Social Security Act, Public Law 89-97. A federal program that pays providers for certain medical and other health services for individuals 65 years of age or older or some disabled persons, regardless of their income. The program has multiple parts, such as hospital insurance (Part A), medical insurance (Part B), and a new prescription portion for medications (Part D).

Narcolepsy. A disorder that affects the control of wakefulness and sleep.

Non-proprietary. A not-for-profit medical center.

Nuclear medicine. A field of medical imaging using invasive radioactive compounds. Sometimes it is considered a subspecialty of radiology.

Obesity. A condition of being overweight that can increase the prevalence of certain health diseases and could lead to increased morbidity.

Occupational Safety and Health Administration (OSHA). An agency of the U.S. Department of Labor that is responsible for issuing and enforcing standards for workplace safety and health.

Occupational therapy. Therapy for individuals who have experienced physical injuries or illnesses, psychological or developmental problems, or problems associated with the aging process.

Oncology. The field of medicine devoted to the study and treatment of cancer.

Ophthalmologist. A licensed physician who treats diseases of the eye often with medications and/or surgery.

Optometrist. Also called Doctor of Optometry (OD). A licensed practitioner concerned with measurement and care of the eyes.

Orthodontist. A dentist who specializes in diagnosing, treating, and preventing dental irregularities through the use of braces and other procedures.

Osteopathic doctor. A licensed physician who usually takes a more general or holistic approach to medicine. Usually, the osteopath physician has extra training in the musculoskeletal system and is more likely to manipulate the patient in a therapeutic manner.

Outpatient. A patient receiving ambulatory care at a hospital or other health facility without being admitted for an overnight stay as an inpatient.

Outpatient laboratory. Medical laboratory that may draw, transport, analyze, and then report the results of patient specimens.

Palliative care. The treatment and care of suffering or symptoms of a serious illness.

Patient-controlled analgesia pump. A device that allows a patient to self-administer prescribed pain medications through an intravenous line.

Pediatric dentistry. The dental specialty for the treatment of children's dental problems.

Periodontitis. A severe, chronic gum disease that comprises bone loss and is permanent. Affected teeth are often lost, resulting in the person needing dentures or teeth implants.

Peritoneal dialysis. A usually self-administered dialysis procedure using an invasive membrane to filter wastes from the blood and body.

Pharmacist. A licensed doctor who prepares, compounds, and dispenses drugs and gives appropriate instructions for their use.

Physiatrist. A physician specialist trained in physical medicine and rehabilitation.

Physical therapy. A rehabilitation process for an injured individual who needs physical assistance in learning to use certain muscle groups or to walk again, or hydrotherapy for burned areas.

Physician's assistant. An individual who extends the service of a supervising physician by taking medical histories, performing physical examinations, and, in circumscribed areas, diagnosing and offering limited treatment to patients.

Podiatrist. Doctor of Podiatric Medicine (PDM). Practitioners who specialize in diagnosing and treating foot and ankle problems.

Positron emission tomography (PET). An nuclear medicine imaging technique, usually of the brain, that produces advanced three-dimensional diagnostic images.

Primary care provider. A doctor trained in general practice or family practice.

Proprietary. A for-profit medical center.

Prosthodontist. A specialist in the restoring of oral function through prostheses and restorations, including dentures, crowns, and dental implants.

Psychiatrist. A licensed physician concerned with providing diagnosis and treatment of mental disorders.

Psychologist. A PhD or PsyD trained in counseling or clinical psychology who engages in the treatment of mental health, performance improvement, or other areas of daily life and health.

Psychotherapy. A general word for treating emotional disorders by talking with a mental health professional. Forms of psychotherapy may be psychoanalysis, art therapy, or behavior therapy.

Public health. A group of agencies and efforts found at all levels of government, including federal, state, and city. These focus on protecting clean air, safeguarding drinking water, and eliminating hazardous waste; inspecting restaurants, food establishments, and grocery stores; inspecting meats, vegetables, and dairy products; safeguarding pharmaceutical products; and safeguarding the workplace. Public health efforts also work to prevent transmittable diseases through education, vaccines, and epidemiology studies.

Recreational therapy. Leisure activities used to maintain and improve an individual's general well-being and health. These activities may include arts and crafts, sports, games, dance, music, or even pet animals.

Rehabilitation medicine. The field of medicine that assists patients in achieving the state of well-being that existed before an accident, injury, heart attack, stroke, cancer, or other illnesses that left the patient in a compromised or altered state of being.

Retirement village. A community comprised of garden-type homes or apartments that allows older people to live independently.

Rheumatology. The medicine of diagnosing and treating chronic rheumatic diseases.

Severe acute respiratory syndrome (SARS). This pulmonary disease, if unchecked, may spread rapidly, as it did in China in the early 21st century.

Sleep apnea. A serious sleep disorder that occurs when the upper airway becomes blocked or obstructed during sleep, often leading to interruptions in breathing.

Speech pathologist. A specialist in the diagnosis and treatment of speech and language disorders as well as the evaluation of oral mechanisms that are responsible for eating and swallowing.

Sports medicine. The prevention, diagnosis, or treatment of physical injuries that are related to sports. Sports medicine may also involve research into the physiological, behavioral, biomechanical, or even biochemical aspects of exercise.

Third-party payer. Any agency or organization that pays or insures a specific package of health or medical expenses on behalf of the beneficiaries or recipients. Examples include but are not limited to Blue Cross/Blue Shield plans, Medicare, Medicaid, and health maintenance organizations.

Transcutaneous electrical nerve stimulation unit (TENS unit). An electronic device used to manage pain by electrodes attached to a small, battery-operated mechanism that sends low-voltage electrical currents through the skin near the area of pain to relieve the pain.

Ultrasound. An imaging procedure used by many practitioners such as obstetricians, cardiologists, or gastroenterologists to noninvasively image and thus detect a range of medical conditions. Usually, ultrasound images are associated with images of the unborn fetus.

Urgent care centers. Medical facilities that are designed for walk-in patients who require timely treatment for injuries or illnesses that are not severe enough to necessitate a trip to a hospital emergency department.

Virtual colonoscopy. A computed tomography procedure that produces three-dimensional images of the colon to diagnose colon and bowel disease.

Virtual office. This is a way to interface with a physician without the need to drive to the physician's office. Questions can be posed or symptoms relayed, and in turn low-cost confidential medical advice is rendered.

Wellness. A state of complete physical, mental, and social well being, not merely the absence of disease or infirmity (World Health Organization's definition of health).

Work hardening. An area of physical medicine that is designed to get an injured worker ready to return to the workplace through a specific formulation of patient appropriate tasks and/or exercises.

World Health Organization. An agency of the United Nations that acts as a coordinating authority for international health.

Zygote intrafallopian transfer. A procedure to transfer fertilized eggs into a woman's fallopian tubes, rather than the uterus, through use of a laparoscope.

Appendix B

Outside the Hospital: Useful URLs

American College of Healthcare Executives	http://www.ache.org
American Hospital Association	http://www.aha.org
American Medical Association	http://www.ama-assn.org
American Nurses Association	http://www.nursingworld.org
American Osteopathic Association	http://www.osteopathic.org
Bioethics.net	http://www.bioethics.net
Centers for Disease Control and Prevention	http://www.cdc.gov
Center for Medicare and Medicaid Services	http://www.cms.hhs.gov
Department of Health and Human Services	http://www.hhs.gov
Families USA	http://www.familiesusa.org
Healthcare Financing Administration	http://www.hcfa.org
Health Insurance Portability and Accountability Act (HIPAA)	http://www.hipaa.org
Joint Commission on Accreditation of Healthcare Organizations	http://www.jcaho.org
Medical Group Management Association	http://www.mgma.com
National Center for Health Statistics	http://www.cdc.gov/nchs
National Institutes of Health	http://www.nih.gov
National Library of Medicine	http://www.nlm.nih.gov
Statistical Abstracts of the United States	http://www.census.gov/index.html

Index